Blues * Harp

AN INSTRUCTION METHOD FOR PLAYING THE BLUES HARMONICA
BY TONY "LITTLE SUN" GLOVER I

Oak Publications

New York · London · Sydney · Cologne

Edited for publication by Kristin White

Layout and design by Jean Hammons

International Standard Book Number: 0-8256-0018-9
Library of Congress Catalog Card Number: 65-26579

Distributed throughout the world by Music Sales Corporation:

33 West 60th Street, New York 10023
78 Newman Street, London W1P 3LA
27 Clarendon Street, Artarmon, Sydney NSW 2064
Kölner Strasse 199, D-5000, Cologne 90

CONTENTS

Tony "Little Sun" Glover   Photo by Karen Glover

SPECIAL THANKS TO:

Karen, who read, listened, watched and put up with the general insanity that makes up a book like this....

Spider John, for invaluable help on the diagrams and transcriptions, and without whose checking and double-cross checking this book might have been.....

Kris White, who talked me into writing this in the first place, and helped see it through to print....

Mel Lyman, who turned me on in front...

The people who read this in mss. and offered suggestions other than "forget it Jim"....

Every blues harpman who's blown a note that touched me....

Whoever runs things, for having the tornadoes which were going on all around leave this book alone....

And all the people really too numerous to name who have helped me survive since I became famous (????) and went broke in more ways than one.

Dedicated to

Kenneth Patchen and Sonny Boy Williamson II,

the two greatest poets of our times.

Sonny Boy Williamson II (May 1965) - Just before his death in Helena, Arkansas.

Photo by Chris Strachwitz

1 In Front

A few things here before we get down to business.

If you're expecting this book to teach you how to sound exactly like Sonny Terry, Little Walter, Sonny Boy Williamson, Jimmy Reed, or any other great harp bluesman--forget it--cause it won't do that. What it will do is give you a taste of the background and mechanics of several main styles of blues harp--and the rest'll be up to you.

You probably picked up this book because you heard the sound of mouth harp blues, got turned on and thought, "Hey--that's where it's at--wish I could do it." The fact is you probably can. Most anybody who is willing to work at it can pick up the techniques involved; how long it takes and how good you get depends on you.

But mastering the technique is only the beginning. The actual truth of the blues lies as much in what you say as in how you say it. It's like learning a language--naturally you want to be able to speak it fluently enough to communicate, but even the most polished and correct speaking won't mean a thing to a native if all you're talking about is the pen of his grandmother--dig? Same thing with music--the flashiest, fanciest, fantastic-est mouth harp technique is wasted unless it's used to help tell the story or paint the mood. Mechanics are only a tool. Don't make the mistake of letting them become an end in themselves.

At first, you'll probably model your style after your favorite harpman, and try to sound as much like him as you can--and that's cool, because you need a sound and technique to aim for. But you should look beyond that. Say that Sonny Terry is your man, and you've worked and practiced and sweated until you've come close to his sound--now you can sit back, take a deep breath and grin at yourself. You sound like Sonny. Now why not go the next step and sound like yourself?

After all, Sonny already sounds like Sonny-- and he is Sonny. And you ain't. But you're something he's not--and that's you. You've got your own ideas, scenes and perceptions. Why not play your own sound? That's one thing that nobody else can or will do for you.

In short, dig the techniques and master the mechanics, then use them to tell a story--your own story.

Another thing.

Blues comes from inside. Most anybody can pick up the techniques and learn the language of the blues, but what you say in this language depends on what's inside you. The hard core center of the blues (call it 'soul' or 'balls' or whatever) can't be put on like a coat--it has to come from the inside out. And that's something you'll never learn from any book. Charlie Parker the jazzman said, "If you don't live it, it won't come out your horn." And that's just about where it's at.

One of the best ways to learn the techniques is listen, listen, listen, listen, every chance you get.

Listen to blues sides, go see performers in person. Listen to the changes, the form, the structure. Get the feel of it inside you, so that you know when a chord change is going to come--and why. Get so that you can feel the logic of the progressions without thinking about them. And store away what you hear, because the time will come when you reach for an idea and BAM! it'll be there--if you've done your listening well. Dig the traditional performers. Listen to Sonny Terry with Leadbelly, Little Walter with Muddy Waters, Sonny Boy Williamson with Big Joe Williams--pick whoever you want, but if you want to play blues harp, make sure that you listen to the solid main stream of the blues. Get a good foundation to build on.

To help you understand some points which just can't be explained in words, Folkways has prepared an instruction record (Blues Mouth Harp, FI 8358) for use with this book.

One last thing. You had best decide right now if you want to be known as a "Harmonica Player", or if you actually want to play harp. There are people who like having the name, fame, chance of glory and riches that they think comes from playing at harp --they like the image more than the work. This book wasn't written for them. It's not a short course on how to get invited to the "in" folk-hippie parties and how to get the girls and recording contracts and how to amaze the folklorists in ten easy lessons. It's for people who really want to learn something about making the sound of blues on a mouth harp.

Straight?? Okay, let's get down with it.

2 Back A Ways

Let's get historical. About 4000 years ago in China (give or take a month), Emperor Haungtei devised the first instrument to use vibrating reeds to produce musical tones--which is the basic principle of the present day harmonica, called "French harp" or just plain "harp" by bluesmen. Though the invention of a "harmonica" is credited to Richard Pockrich, an Irishman, and its actual development to a playable instrument to Benjamin Franklin (you know; almanacs, kites in thunderstorms, etc.)--it was nothing like the harmonica of today. They used a series of glass discs of varying sizes which were gently rubbed by the fingertips and the discs revolved in water-- making the tones of the scale.

Nobody has ever quite decided just who invented the harp as we know it today, but the ever-popular Encyclopedia Britannica says that Sir Charles Wheatstone (bridges, etc.) did it in 1829. It was called the "aeolina" and used reeds of different lengths in a metal box. As you moved it back and forth across your lips, blowing on the reeds made it possible to play simple tunes.

Harmonicas were first commercially manufactured in Germany by Fredrich Hotz, who later merged with M. Hohner. This marked the beginning of the largest harmonica and accordion factory in the world.

Parelleled with this is the musical background of the Negro, who had a long history of adopting readily available materials for use as musical instruments. When Negroes were first brought to America, they had an already well-developed musi-

9

cal heritage--and when the elements of the African tradition that survived mingled with the European-based harmonies and rhythms heard here, the result was "blues". Probably the earliest known Afro-American musical form was the "field holler", so called because it was hollered in fields by laborers. The swooping vocal style was closer to African than European tonality and a falsetto voice with gliding, unmouthed tones were often used. Later, on the plantations, the Negroes freely adapted the hymns they heard the whites singing, and the result was the call-and-response choral style that came to be known as "spirituals".

Following the civil war, Negroes got hold of instruments discarded by army bands and taught themselves to play them. Naturally, they used these instruments as they used their voices, playing in an almost vocal-sounding style. Dig some early Dixieland and you'll see. As guitars became available in the south (probably due to mail-order catalogues and low prices), the Negro used them as well, again adapting techniques to get the African-descended "responsive voice" sound. Often, especially in the delta country in Mississippi, they fretted the strings with jacknives or bottlenecks, producing tones that could bend, slur, and whine, following the singers' flowing vocal style with ease. (This technique is an outgrowth of one of the simplest of all instruments: a strand of baling wire was stapled to a wall, two spools were put under it (one at top and one at bottom) and moved to tighten the wire, raising its pitch to the level desired. It was played by plucking, and a bottleneck was used to fret the wire, raising or lowering the pitch at will. This skeleton was once very popular in the rural south, according to blues researcher and collector, Harold Courlander.)

And then came the simplest and cheapest instrument of all--the harmonica.

It was loosely related to the African cane fife or quill pipes, and of all manufactured instruments it was easily the most vocal-sounding. It had the advantages of being small and easy to carry anywhere, it didn't have strings to break or valves to repair, and it was fairly easy to learn to play since no fingering patterns were needed.

Here again, the Negroes used their own techniques to get the uniquely expressive vocal sound, a style of playing which demands a much higher degree of creativity in the mechanics of playing than the jazz or "classical" harmonica styles which whites developed in later years.

By 1930, the harmonica was tremendously popular. Production was in the neighborhood of 25 million. Many high schools and colleges had harmonica bands--the Philadelphia Harmonica Band traveled widely in the U.S., giving successful concerts and recitals.

Up until World War II harmonicas cost only about 50 cents. During the war they were almost totally unobtainable, and when they did become available again the price had risen to about $2.50. Classical music played on the harmonica became popular and such composers as Darius Milhaud and Villa-Lobos were writing especially for it. A few small harmonica groups appeared on the entertainment scene, and pop recordings featuring harmonica were heard. In 1950 the American Federation of Musicians declared the harmonica a legitimate instrument, and invited (hah) all players to join.

The harp was in.

3

Blues Harp - Some History and Some People

The harp was much in evidence as a part of a musical tradition which flourished in the rural south in the 1920's and 30's--the jug band. These bands, which played on street corners, in saloons, and at country suppers, usually used banjo, guitar, washboard, and kazoo, and sometimes fiddle, jugs, and harp. But most often the harp was used in these bands for melodic-rhythmic support, with much of the playing being done in the upper register so that the sound would carry over the booming jugs and thumping rhythm backing.

The earliest evidence that I've heard of the harp being used as a solo or lead instrument were the recordings made by George "Bullet" Williams, in the late 20's. The only information I have is that Bukka White (the rediscovered Mississippi blues great) says that Williams was his first wife's sister's husband (got that?), and that Williams is probably dead or insane now, since he had a habit of drinking shoe polish strained through bread. But his harp style was fierce and moving--he played with a frightening intensity. In the following years, many excellent harp bluesmen have appeared on record, but a few stand out as trendsetters and innovators.

The most country-or "folk"-styled harpman still active is Sonny Terry, who was born Saunders Tedell near Durham, North Carolina in 1911. His father, a farmer, taught Sonny the basics of harp playing. When Sonny was left almost totally blind from two separate accidents, he left home at 16, playing on street corners to make a living. In 1934 he met a guitarist known as Blind Boy Fuller, who was doing the same shot. They teamed up, traveled together and even cut a few records together in New York in 1937 and in South Carolina in 1938. In 1939 Sonny was a featured attraction at the gigantic "Spirituals to Swing" concert presented at Carnegie Hall by John Hammond. In 1940, Fuller died of a kidney ailment, and Sonny teamed up with Brownie McGhee, his partner from then to the present. Musically Sonny has run the whole gamut--from folk beginnings to folk-oriented recordings with Leadbelly and Woody Guthrie, from early commercial blues sides with Fuller to R&B sides with Brownie in the 40's and 50's --from street corners in the south to concert stages all across the world. Today he is probably the most widely-known harmonica bluesman.

Another highly influential blues singer-harpist was the Chicago-based Sonny Boy Williamson I. Although he was born (1921) near Jackson, Tennessee, his style was more in the city blues vein than the country, and when he moved to Chicago in the early 30's, he worked as a sideman with many different bluesmen. In the late 30's he began to record as a featured artist, fronting his own band--which usually consisted of piano, guitar, bass and drums. These recordings laid the groundwork for the Chicago style of R&B that dominated the blues scene in the late 40's and early 50's. Sonny Boy (real name: John Lee Williamson) used country or folk based material, but citified it in arrangements more palatable to the urban, industrialized Negro. This type of "arranged" country blues, with a heavy beat added was his main contribution. His style of "choked" harp that broke into a half-moan, half-scream was tremendously popular and influential. He was murdered with an icepick in 1948. Almost every harpman to record after him owes a good deal to his style.

The next major trendsetter was Louisiana-born (1930) Little Walter (real name, Marion Walter Jacobs). His family moved to Chicago when he was a youth and while still in his teens he started playing with such bluesmen as Big Bill Broonzy and Muddy Waters, even though he was occasionally thrown out of the clubs because of his age. He was influenced by Sonny Boy, and one of his earliest solo recordings (with Muddy Waters on guitar and Sunnyland Slim on piano) was an outright attempt to imitate the then best-selling Williamson sound. Later however, he evolved his own style which was a cross between city and country styles and which fitted in perfectly with the band of Muddy Waters, with whom he worked and recorded for several years. Muddy was one of the founders, if not the founder, of Chicago-styled R&B; his material was drawn from his Mississippi delta background, but had an updated sound--he used electric guitar, bottleneck style, bass, drums, and Little Walter on amplified harmonica. As far as I can discover, Little Walter was the first to record using this technique. The method was simple: he had his own amplifier and PA mike--he cupped both the mike and harp in his hands--with his own amplifier he had complete control of his sound. The amplification was born of necessity--the piercing guitars and drums completely drowned out unamplified harp--but it also added a new dimension, because of the various tone and echo effects built into the amps. Also, amplified harp could be used as a lead instrument, even with full volume backing. Little Walter was the first bluesman to use a chromatic harmonica regularly-- up till then the Marine Band was the most widely used model. When amplified the chromatic gave a deeper organ-like sound. It had the advantage of being able to be played in any key (theoretically), but the disadvantage of stiffer reeds, making the "bending" of notes, so necessary for blues, much harder. But Little Walter mastered it and is one of the most musically creative of the blues harpmen. After leaving Muddy he fronted his own band, often doing instrumental numbers with a complex and inventive structure. He is still active (he toured in England recently and was surprised by the many followers he found there), though his more recent recordings tend more towards more commercially saleable R&R. His style has spawned many followers and every R&B harpman owes a good deal to him.

The next most notable distinctive harpman is not mainly a harpman at all--Jimmy Reed (born in Leland Mississippi around 1928) is mostly a singer-guitarist. But his use of the harp as a laconic accompanying voice is widely imitated. He tends to concentrate on "high" notes, in simple melodic riffs, but the intensely-voiced harp sound works perfectly with his overall sound of snaky, floating, head blues.

By far the best of the contemporary singer bluesharpists was Sonny Boy Williamson II. He was born in Glendora, Mississippi, in 1897 (according to him), or Tallahatchie, in 1909 (according to his passport.) His real name was Willie "Rice" Miller, and his claim to be the "original" Sonny Boy is true in the sense that he is the older of the two. In 1938 he was broadcasting over station KFFA in Helena, Ark. on a show called "Sonny Boy's King Biscuit Flour Show", and although he claims to have recorded in the late 30's, the first known recordings by him appeared in 1951 on the Trumpet label, which was based in Jackson, Miss. Some of his sidemen on these sides were the well-known guitarists Elmore James and B. B. King. With the success of these recordings he toured more widely in the north, settling in St. Louis in 1959. A year later he was working regularly in the Chicago area. He had a fantastic, groovy, splendid, and delicious technique, made all the more effective by his sparing use of flashiness--he was in total control of his instrument at all times. Recently he toured England and Europe, and got such a warm welcome that he considered living there for good. His songs were often pure poetry, both in words and music, and his work influenced many of the younger blues harpmen, especially in the British R&B groups. On May 24, 1965, he died of a heart attack on a gig in Arkansas. When he died, he left a hole in the world that won't be easily, if ever, filled. His records remain as evidence of his pure, intense and beautiful reflections of the world he lived in, a world maybe made a little richer from the truths he told. He put his whole soul into his sound...his death marks the end of an era. I feel sorry for everybody who never heard him, and sorrier for those that did and missed the point.

Jr. Wells (left) - Chicago harpman who worked with
Muddy Waters and has made several solo records.

Photo by Bob Koester
Courtesy of Delmark Records

Other good harpmen include Junior Wells, James Cotton, and Shakey Walter Horton, all of whom have worked at one time or another with Muddy Waters. Others in the Chicago style are Billy Boy (William) Arnold and Snooky Pryor. Howling Wolf (born Chester Burnett in Aberdeen, Miss. in 1910) plays harp in a style much like that of Sonny Boy I--who taught him. There are many harpmen who record for the Excello label in Louisiana; the better ones are Lazy Lester (Johnson), Slim Harpo (James Moore) and "Ole Sonny Boy"...their styles vary from the sound of Sonny Boy to Little Walter influences, but they usually have a slightly more "country" flavor.

The above list is by no means complete, and I'm hip that many people won't agree with my choices (write your own book, sorehead)--but it's a cross-section of the people currently available on record.

In the last few years, recordings of whites playing blues harp have begun to show up (it's been happening for years but the record companies and general public got hip only recently). In the U.S. most of it is in the folk vein, though there are several good white R&B harpmen on the way up. In England, the recreation of traditional R&B material has been going on for some time, and the popularity of the Beatles has helped draw general attention to some of the funkier, R&B-styled groups, such as the Rolling Stones and Manfred Mann, who often use harp backing.

What it amounts to is that blues is no longer the exclusive property of the Negro, in the same way that the Top-40 charts are no longer the exclusive property of the whites. There is a tremendous amount of interchange going on all the time and it'll be a wig to see where it ends up. At present, there are probably many more white youths than Negro playing blues (R&B has become a pop-infiltrated sound best called Rock & Blues)--so in one way or another the blues tradition will survive. The history of blues harp is still being written. All you got to do is listen.

A **blues** veteran, Big Mama Thornton is one of the outstanding female harmonica players.

Photo courtesy of M. Hohner

4

Choosing Your Ax

What kind of harp should you get? The possibilities are almost limitless: there are several brands on the market, but the most readily available and most reliable harps are made by M. Hohner,-- they're almost like Bell Telephone--but their monopoly is by no means complete yet. In the Hohner line you can go from the "Little Lady" model, with eight reeds selling for fifty cents, to the "Chord Harmonica" (which is actually two harps hinged together) with a total of 384 reeds, selling for $150.

But neither of those is much good for blues. The model I suggest, and the one used by most bluesmen, and the one on which all the diagrams, etc., in this book are based, is the Hohner "Marine Band" #1896 model, which sells for about $2.50. The Marine Band has ten single holes with twenty reeds and covers a range of three octaves--it comes in all keys generally used.(i.e., A, B-flat, C, D, E, F and G. They can also be found in the key of B, but those are a little rare.)

Another model the "Old Standby"--with the same reed and key setup, sells for about fifty cents less than the Marine Band--but the longer life and durability of the Marine Band makes the difference well worth paying. The model known as "Auto-Valve" harp often tempts buyers. It's actually two harps, one above the other, and it's advertised as making playing easier--more volume with less breath--but I find that for blues it's mostly useless. And the same thing is true for the various "Echo" models which have tremolo reeds, with a 'quivering' sound.

The big Marine Band (#365), with fourteen holes and 28 reeds is sometimes used (Sonny Boy II cut several sides playing it). It sells for about $4, and comes in only two keys, C or G. It has a tone setup of reeds about the same as the smaller model but is a little more awkward as a blues instrument. However, it might be a good harp to keep in mind for the future--the one in C tuning has some beautiful low notes which work groovy for low-down, easy lead work.

Later on you may want a chromatic harp, particularly if you plan to do R&B band work, but if you are going to play mostly folk and city blues the Marine Band is the best. But if you want a chromatic, try the Chromonica #260 made by Hohner. Since you can play a chromatic in any key, it comes in only two tunings--C and G again. The #260 has ten holes and 40 reeds, covers a range of three chromatic octaves, and sells for about $10. If you really want to go all the way and get that big monster that Little Walter uses, it's the "64 Chromonica" with sixteen

holes, 64 reeds and a range of four full chromatic octabes--it retails for about $20. But unless you plan to do a lot of amplified work where you need a heavy sound forget it--I've had one for years and only played it three times.

So the best bet for a starter is the #1896 Marine Band. Check out your nearby music dealer, or write for a complete catalogue to M. Hohner, Andrews Road, Hicksville, L.I., New York.

Which key? If you plan to be playing with a guitar a lot try an A-tuned harp, (it works with a guitar played in E, and E is the most popular blues key for the guitar). Or if you plan to do a lot of solo work, C harp is a good buy--its reeds are in the middle ranges and are easy to work with. If you're serious about harp, you'll eventually want to get all keys, but in front you can make it pretty well with A and C. Cool???

5 Harps - How They Work
And How To Work Them

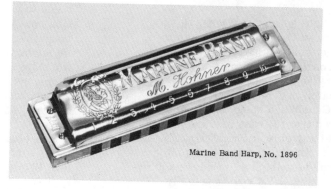

Marine Band Harp, No. 1896

Figure 1

Pictured above is the Marine Band harp, on which the material in this following section is based. If you were to take the covering plates off, you'd see that the guts of it consist of two metal plates, which form the top and bottom of the box, closed entirely by wood on three sides, with ten holes on the remaining side. Into each of these metal plates ten channels are cut. (See the diagram below--in both the top and bottom views the low notes are to the left and the high notes to the right.) Thin strips of metal called reeds are attached at one end, so that each can vibrate freely in the channels cut for it. Notice that on the top (A), the reeds are placed inside the box, and attached at the end towards the mouthpiece. On the bottom (B), they are placed outside the box, on top of the plate, attached on the end away from the mouthpiece. With this set-up, you can get two tones from one hole.

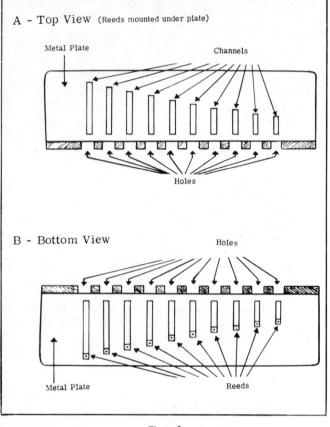

A - Top View (Reeds mounted under plate)

Metal Plate

Channels

Holes

B - Bottom View

Holes

Metal Plate

Reeds

Figure 2

If you blow into hole #1 (far left), the air will escape through one of the channels cut into the plate, since it can't get out anywhere else. In this case it will go out through the top side (A above) and as it escapes it will cause the reed to vibrate, producing a tone with a pitch in direct relation to the length of the reed. (Consider a piano one time-- you've probably noticed that the bass or "low" strings are much longer than the treble or "high" strings. The longer a reed or string is, the deeper its pitch-- the shorter it is, the higher its pitch. Or take a guitar--when you fret a string, what you're actually doing is shortening the length of the part of it that vibrates and produces the tone which raises the tone pitch. Straight?)

Now as you're blowing into hole #1, the air escapes through the top channel, causing the reed to vibrate outward. At the same time, the reed in the channel of the bottom plate is pulled in, towards the inside of the box--but it doesn't vibrate. Instead, it just closes off the channel, so that you get just a single tone--the tone of the top reed.

If you suck or draw in on the same hole, the bottom reed (far left, B) would vibrate out as the air is pulled in, while the top reed stays shut, not vibrating--so again, only the tone of the vibrating reed is heard. In this way, you get 20 tones from a ten-hole harp, and can play both blowing out and drawing in. Okay? (It isn't absolutely necessary to understand the above to be able to play--but it's nice to know the "why" of it too.)

So we've got 20 separate tones available through the ten holes--two per hole--one by blowing, the other by drawing or sucking (make a Freudian choice of terms). Now study the diagram below.

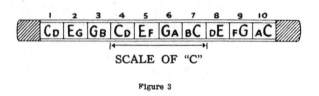

SCALE OF "C"

Figure 3

Dig first off that it's for a harp tuned in C. The "Blow" notes are the large capital letters, the "Draw" notes are the smaller capital letters. (In the 1st hole, C is the blow note, D is the draw-- etc.) This, and all other #1896 Marine Band harps are set up in diatonic tuning--which just means that it's set up on the eight-tone scale; do, re, mi, fa, so, la, ti, and do again. Notice that the only complete scale starts on the #4 hole and runs through the #7 hole. The first three holes contain only a partial scale--but it is this particular setup that makes blues harp possible. Harps tuned this way, when played in keys other than the one they're tuned to, produce chords that can't be got otherwise.

But that's jumping ahead a little. (Any of you who know how to play harp in the key that it's tuned to can skip ahead to the "Crossed Harp" section now.) Those of you who took my advice and bought an A harp are probably cussing me out for using a diagram of a C harp. Well, relax-- the relationships between tones are the same in Marine Band harps, no matter what they key. An A harp, for instance, would be set up like this: #1 hole; blow-A, draw-B, #2 hole; blow-C#, draw-E, #3 hole; blow-E, draw-G#, followed by a complete scale starting with A as a blow note in hole #4, and so on the rest of the way. And it's the same for all keys: you just skip a tone between the blow and draw notes in the #2 and #3 holes, repeat the draw note in hole #2 as a blow note in hole #3, and start the complete octave as the blow note in hole #4. Simple, ?? And any of you wise guy trained musicians who are saying "what about the sharps and flats in other keys?"--cool it, because that's taken care of. The reeds are already tuned to the right pitch. In an A harp for example, the appropriate reeds are pretuned to C#, F# and G#-- so you don't have to sweat it.

If you have a harp other than one in C tuning it'd be a good idea to make a diagram of the tone layout like the one above. Just follow along, starting with the note your harp is tuned to as the blow note in hole #1, and go according to the layout for the C harp. Don't worry about the exercises to come either-- the relationships between tones will stay the same, even though the actual pitch will be different.

Okay, let's assume that this is the first time you've ever tried to play harp at all. How do you hold it? The easiest way is to hold it whichever way

18

is most comfortable for you. But there's one thing to consider—are you right-or left-handed? If you're right-handed, you'll probably want to hold the harp in your left hand, with the low notes to the left, your thumb below and the other fingers on top. Like this:

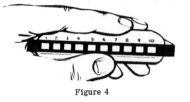

Figure 4

This leaves your right hand free to form a cup with your left, over the harp, and you can vibrate your hand back and forth, opening and closing the cup to produce "wah-wah" and tremolo effects. If you're left-handed, you'll probably want to reverse it—that is, hold it in your right hand, upside down (with the low notes to the right), and cup with your left hand. In either case the important thing is to have it so that you can get a completely closed cup over the lower notes (where most of the rhythm and tremolo effects happen).

On the other foot, though, I've known right-handed harpmen who held it upside down (low notes to the right) and got along okay, so I guess it all depends on which way you pick it up the first time. Do what's right for you.

Now that you've practiced holding your harp for awhile, you're ready to blow. We'll start off with some simple, rather insipid little tunes. Although playing melody probably won't be of much use to you in playing blues, the practice of getting a simple single clear tone is good for you. (The tunes below are diagrammed in a system invented by Thomas Hart Benton, the painter, and are used by permission of M. Hohner, Inc.) The notes above the holes are for a C harp, but if you have a different key just ignore them and use the hole numbers only. The system works like this: the number shows which hole you use, the direction of the arrows shows whether you blow or draw (an arrow pointing up ▲ means blow, down ▼ means draw), and the length of the arrows shows the relative length of time the tones should be held. Try this little gem one time:

HOT CROSS BUNS

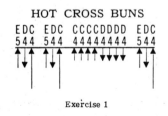

Exercise 1

Try to get <u>single</u> tones—a clear unblurred note from each hole. It may be a little hard at first,

but you can do it. There are two main methods—one is the "tongue-blocking method" shown below.

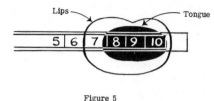

Figure 5

Your lips surround four holes, your tongue blocks the three on the right, leaving the hole on the left open for sound. If you do it this way you'll be cool on the lower notes at the left of the harp, and that's where a lot of the action is for blues harp.

I didn't learn this way myself, and I find it a bit awkward—but it's a good thing to know—especially if you plan to play chromatic—tongue-blocking is the main way to "bend" notes on a chromatic harp. I was lazier—I just pursed my lips down so that they only opened to one hole at a time. Probably best for beginning would be to learn both ways and pick your favorite—they both come in handy.

Try this one time:

MARY HAD A LITTLE LAMB

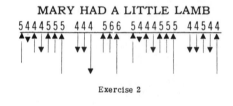

Exercise 2

Or get a little fancier and swing with this:

ROW, ROW, ROW YOUR BOAT

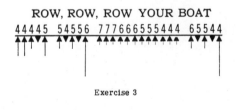

Exercise 3

Or get down to the real nitty-gritty:

THREE BLIND MICE

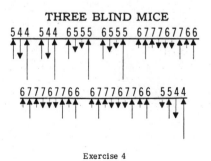

Exercise 4

19

By now you've probably noticed something--all of the tunes above are in holes #4 through #7. That's because those holes contain the only complete octave available on the Marine Band harp. (Remember that on a C harp the F and A notes are missing in the first octave. Later on, in crossed-harp style, you'll learn how to bend other notes to make the missing F and A tones. But for now, just practice getting around on the notes available without any hassle.) Try "Skip To My Lou"--it's folksy.

SKIP TO MY LOU

Exercise 5

Although you may feel that you're wasting your time with these dumb little melodies, you're not--not as long as you concentrate on getting single tones, and getting used to getting around on the harp. As far as breathing goes, just do what comes natur-ally- you'll find that you may be doing some breathing around the harp, some through it and some through your nose--just let your body take care of itself. The only real thing you can do about your breathing now is to cut out smoking--cause wailing all night takes a lot of wind.

Farther on you'll notice some rhythmic patterns written out in standard musical notation--but don't get up tight if you can't read music. The same patterns are given in a modified version of this arrow method as well. For that matter, there has not yet been any written music for blues harp--at least none I know about--and all the harp bluesmen I know have done pretty good without ever being able to read music. So the examples written in regular music notation are for those who already know how to read music--but the rest of you (which includes me) don't really need to learn.

Now what you've been doing so far is playing first position, or "straight" harp--that is, harp in the key that it is tuned to. As you can see, it's good for playing melodies--but that's just about it--"straight" harp has its limitations. A lot of classical and popular harmonicists use this position, as do those who play in the country-western-hillbilly Guthrie-Elliott-Dylan vein. Some jug band tunes use straight harp, and Jimmy Reed works out with it regularly too, but by far the most flexible and widely used position for blues harp is the following--"cross harp."

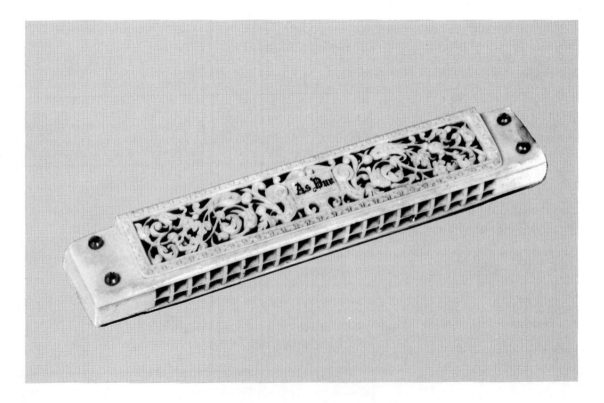

6

Cross Harp - "Why"

First off, some theory. You won't have to
memorize it all to be able to play, but it won't hurt to
know the reasons why it works like it does. You
know about the three main chords used in most folk
and blues music progressions, right? Of course the
music is a lot more complicated than just three
chords on a guitar, but these chords (Tonic: the
same as the key you're playing in, say C for example; Subdominant: a fourth above the tonic, F in the
key of C; and Dominant: a fifth above the tonic, G in
the key of C) are the basic foundations for most all
blues, and usually the many and varied patterns and
tones are built on or around these three main chords.

Say that you're playing a blues on a guitar
in the key of C--the progression (at its simplest)
would go about like this:

(C-tonic)
My baby told me she was leaving town,

     (F-Subdominant)   (C)
Yes, my baby told me she was leaving town,

(G-dominant)   (F)   (C)
Now she gone, ain't nothin' good around.

If you were to accompany this progression
with a C harp, playing in the key of C (straight or 1st
position), it would go like this (again, at the simplest):

1st line: Blow #4 hole (C)
2nd line: Draw #5 hole (F) and Blow 4th hole (C)
3rd line: Blow #3 hole (G), Draw 5th hole (F) and
                Blow 4th hole (C)

You dig, it works. Doesn't sound great, but it works. You'll notice that you have to be careful to get only single notes, especially on the F tone, or you get some pretty horrible discords.

And you'll also notice that of your three chords, you have to blow to get two of them (C and G), and only one (F) is a draw note. So what? So this--to play blues harp you need to be able to "bend" notes to make halftones and slurs--and it's at least 134 times easier to bend a draw note than a blow note--especially on the lower and heavier reeds.

Some of you may have checked back to Figure 3, page 18, and dug that that the dominant tone in the above progression (G) is available as a draw note in the #2 hole as well as a blow note in #3, like we used above. So you figure it's straight, you got two draw notes and only one blow to work with--but there's a hassle: use it that way and the draw notes are on the dominant and subdominant tones--but the chords you really want to bend, wail, and slur on are the dominant and tonic...which can't both be got as draw notes in first position. Another drawback to using first position for blues is that it's pretty hard to find chords on the harp that sound good with the guitar. You have to stick mostly to single notes-- and the wailing chord sound is an important part of most blues harp styles.

So, we got to find another position, another way to play a harp where we can get both the tonic and dominant notes of the guitar key as draw notes, and also a position where chords are possible. Go back to Figure 3. (Remember now that this relationship is the same for all keys--the same notes are skipped or repeated in the same holes in the same order always.) There is a reason why those notes are skipped, by the way. If a complete scale was started in the #1 hole and carried on up, in order, (Blow-C, Draw-D, Blow-E, Draw-F etc.) the scale would end all right with the next octave (the next C note) being a blow tone--but the draw note in that hole would be B, and not D as it was in the first hole. (Dig holes #4-#7.) The people who make

harps decided that this kind of setup, carried out all through the harp would be too confusing for people playing "straight" harp, so they set it up the way you see in the diagram. This way, the main notes in the key of C (C, E and G) are always available as blow notes, all through the harp. This setup is what makes cross harp possible.

All that "cross harp" means is playing a harp in a key different from the one that it's tuned to. Notice how the G tone is repeated in holes #2 and #3? That's useful. And notice how you get a chord either blowing or drawing on holes #2 and #3? That's useful--we need all the chords we can get. Maybe a C harp played in the key of G might work... let's check it out.

Here's another simple blues progression, this time with the guitar in the key of G:

    (G-tonic)
I'm evil, been evil all my days,

    (C-subdominant)   (G)
Well, I'm evil, been evil all my days,

(D-dominant)   (C)   (G)
Seems like evil gonna carry me to my grave.

Now, to accompany this progression, playing a C harp in the key of G, you work it out like this (once again, at the basic simplest):

    1st line: Draw #2 hole (G)
    2nd line: Blow #4 hole (C) and Draw #2 hole (G)
    3rd line: Draw #4 hole (D), Blow #4 hole (C) and Draw #2 hole (G)

And it works okay. Check further and you dig that the tonic and dominant are both draw notes, so they can be "bent", and if you play holes #2 and #3 (drawing in) during the tonic part of the progression you can hear that you get a tonic chord on the harp--and that's where it's at!

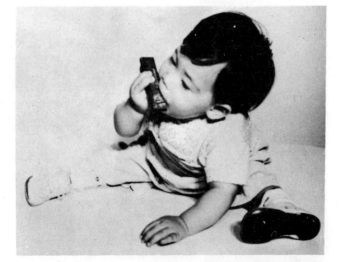

Baby with harp - blue period.   Photo courtesy of M. Hohner

That's how "cross", "suck" or second position harp works--you play harp in the same key as the guitar, but you use a harp which is tuned to a key a fourth above the key of the guitar.   Here's an easy way to remember the cross: *you always use a harp tuned in the key of the subdominant chord of the guitar key.* (Or another way--use a harp that has the same tone in the #2 hole draw as the guitar key.)

And this relationship holds for all keys. Dig the chromatic scale below (chromatic means twelve tones--like one octave on the piano, using both the black and white keys):

CHROMATIC SCALE

C C# D D# E F F# G G# A A# B

Say that you want to play cross harp with a guitar in the key of E--count up five steps (or tones) beginning on F and you land on A--which is the subdominant chord for the key of E, and the key of the harp you'd use. Or say the guitar is in A. Count five, starting with A# (which is the same as B-flat)--when you reach the end on the right, go back to the left and continue from there, and you land on D--the subdominant tone in the key of A--and the pitch of the harp you use. And so on for all seven diatonic keys. (Remember that diatonic is eight-toned scale--like one octave on the white keys of a piano--C, D, E, F,

G, A, B and C again.) You'll notice that if the guitar is in F, when you count up five steps on the diagram you land on A#--but it's cool, A# is the same as B-flat, and they do make B-flat harps. But you'll also notice if you experiment some that guitars in sharped keys don't work out--for instance the key of D# means a G# harp should be used--and there ain't no such animal. But how many guitar players do you know who work out that often in D#?? (Third and fourth position harp make it possible to accompany sharped keys, but for now, you'll do fine with the seven keys available--in fact you'll probably never use all seven.)

All the above information is based on the assumption that the guitar is in concert pitch (that is, with the E strings tuned to E etc.) Some guitar players (especially 12-string men) prefer to tune below concert pitch to lessen the tension on the wood. Farther on, you'll find tables which show which harp to use with which key guitar (saves all that counting) with tables for low tunings as well. Got you covered, baby.

And that pretty well covers the basic idea behind cross harp. Like I said, you don't have to know all this theory before you're ready to blow (I was playing for three years before I ever heard of a subdominant chord)--but the more you know about your ax, the more you can do with it. Now you know "why"--here's some of the how.

Jesse "Lone Cat" Fuller plays harmonica, guitar, kazoo, and home-made instruments, and sings, too. He is the composer of "San Francisco Bay Blues".

7

Cross Harp - "How"

Chords and Tone Techniques

One of the first things is to learn where to find the three main tones--the tonic, subdominant and dominant and to get used to playing harp in this position so that even without a guitar around you naturally play crossed whenever you pick up a harp.   It might help to diagram it first, like this:

STRAIGHT HARP (first position)

tonic   subdominant   dominant

4↑   5↓   3↑

CROSSED HARP (second position)

tonic   subdominant   dominant

2↓   4↑   4↓

The arrows pointing up mean blow, pointing down mean draw. If the technical terms hang you up, substitute chords of a guitar key--say E. Instead of tonic, subdominant and dominant, you'd have E, A and B^7.

If you've done your blues listening well, you should know what the 12-bar form sounds like, and where the changes would come in any verse of a song. If you don't have a partner who can lay down twelve bars on a guitar for you, sit down by yourself and blow your way through a chorus on the harp--keeping in mind the tune you're playing with in your

25

head. Or work with records. Get so that you can find the right holes at the right times by instinct and feel instead of by counting. Hit all your notes cleanly, so that you get clear and single tones without unintentional wavering. Later on you'll want to hit chords, slur notes and use a wavering effect--but it's a hell of a lot easier to add those effects when you want them than to try and take them out when you want to play pure.

The only way you can do this is by playing playing playing. There ain't any shortcuts. Play as often as you can. But I don't mean to sit down and work out six hours at a time--it'd be better to play for fifteen minutes four times a day than for an hour once a day--if you try to do too much at once, you get to a point where everything sounds like frozen mush clattering through your neighbor's skylight. Of course, how much and how often you play is up to you--but don't overdo it. Learning to play shouldn't be a race or an endurance test--the main idea is to ball. You got to work some so that you _can_ ball--but if you let it get to where it's all work and no kicks you're missing the whole point of making music.

Once you've got so that you're fairly well at home in cross position, try working out some of the following ideas:

On the tonic tone, open up your lips and tongue so that both holes #2 and #3 are open. Draw in and you've got part of a chord. (On an A harp it'd be an E chord, on a C harp a G chord and so on.) You should be holding the harp like the drawing in Figure 4--with the low note side towards the palm of the hand holding it. Now put the heel of your other hand up against the hand holding the harp so that the fingers of your "free" hand can come up and close over the fingers of your harp hand--in other words, make a cup. Now open the cup up (keep the heels of your hands together and pivot from there), draw in on holes #2 and #3 and vibrate your hand back and forth, opening and closing the cup rapidly. Dig the tremolo sound you get? (The faster you vibrate your hand, the faster the tremolo.) Now try moving your whole hand back and forth--use your elbow as the pivot point. You'll get a slightly fuller sound that way, and a different-sounding tremolo. Experiment around and see the various ways to do it and how they work. Keep in mind it works best if you hold the harp so that you can completely close it off when you make the cup.

Now blow _out_ thru holes #2 and #3 and you get another chord (or part of one, actually). On an A harp it'd be part of an A chord, on a C, part of a C chord etc. Now add the tremolo effect. Now alternate back and forth between blow-draw blow -draw, always ending on draw. (You're playing crossed, remember??) Try it both fast and slow. Experiment with the tremolo sound.

Before you can get any solid chord rhythms going, you have to be able to "kill" or cut off chords sharply. (A chick I know calls this "making it quack.") Try it on the draw chord on holes #2 and #3. Draw your breath in very sharply, almost like a gasp, but harder--and at the same time pull your

tongue back and away from the harp, towards the roof of your mouth, near the gums. If you can't get it, try it first without a harp. Start with your tongue where it naturally is, just sort of laying around your mouth. Now open your mouth a little and suck a chunk of air in--then sharply bring your tongue up to your gums as if it were scooping the air up. Hit the gums hard enough so that you can hear a little "hut" sound. Now try it again with the harp. You may not be able to get a complete "kill" at first, but it'll come in time. Work at this--it's important to be able to kill a note or chord at any time. Get it so that the "kill" is sharp--it should stop abruptly and not sound blurred or fuzzy. The reeds will echo for a split second after you've cut off the air (especially on big G harps) but don't sweat that--it's cool as long as you've cut it off _sharp_.

Now try cutting off the blow chord. Your tongue does about the same thing (don't try to force it, it should come fairly naturally. Your body is a lot hipper than you'd expect it to be--give it its head and it'll learn new tricks faster than a new dog all by its own self), but your breath explodes out in a short burst--as if you were shooting a poison dart through a blow-gun, or like a spitball, if you'd rather.

Work on this until you can get sharp "kill" sounds on both the blow and draw chords. Once you've got them sharp and clean, let's play with a sort of train rhythm. (All harmonica players got to know how to sound like trains. It's a rule.)

Try talking through the harp--what I mean: shape your mouth and tongue to form the words as you usually would when talking, but leave your vocal chords out of it--let the harp reeds make the sound. On the in (draw) chord say "dit dit" through the harp, cutting off the air after each "dit". On the out (blow) chord say "dah dah", again cutting off for a fraction of a second after each "dah".

To write it out, we'll have to make some changes in the arrow system. We need another way to tell time--how long a note is in relation to the other notes. Instead of having arrows of different lengths to mark time differences (this setup would get pretty unintelligible with blues rhythms), we'll use a bar, placed over the notes--like the lines over letters in English classes showing long "a's"--for

the time unit. For example: $\overline{dit\text{-}dit}$ $\overline{dah}$ $\overline{\overline{dah}}$.

(In standard rhythmic notation: ♩♩ ♩ ♪)

Remember that it's the _number_ of lines above a syllable that determines the length of time you hold it. The length of the lines has no significance.

In the above, a single line represents the basic unit--this unit can be any length you want to make it (depends on how fast you're playing) but it's your basic reference. In this example, the "dah" note has a single line over it, so it's your reference-

-or one unit. Since the two "dit" notes together have a single line over both of them, it means that each of them takes half as long to play as the "dah" note-- you play both "dits" in the same amount of time as you play the single "dah" note. The second "dah" has two lines, over it, indicating two time units which means that it's held twice as long as the "dah" note. Remember that a unit can be any length of time that you want it to be--but the relationship between the length of notes stays the same whether you hold a unit for a tenth of a second or for a full second... okay??

Now let's get back to a train-type rhythm. Like this:

(Use holes #2 and #3)

dit-dit dah-dah dit-dit dah-dah
 ▼ ▼ ▲ ▲ ▼ ▼ ▲ ▲

dit-dit dah-dah etc.
 ▼ ▼ ▲ ▲

The time here is simple--a dit dit chord is equal to a dah/dah chord. Tapping your foot helps to keep rhythm--at first you may want to tap on every mark (or time unit)--later on it may be easier to tap on every other mark, or on every fourth mark. It depends again on which is most comfortable and works best for you. (Myself, I tap out afterbeats--which drives my partners nuts--but it works for me.) Try the above slowly at first, then gradually build up speed. Groovy, huh?? Fool around with it until it comes naturally, so that you can switch from draw to blow, draw to blow without thinking about it, and get the rhythm going good and steady.

Try adding a whistle sound. After a phrase ending on a blow chord, move on up the harp to holes #3 and #4 and draw in--and at the same time use your cupped hands for the vibrating tremolo effect. Then blow out through the same holes (still with the tremolo working), then draw in again, then blow out once more and return to the rhythm chords. Your whistle chords should last about three or four times as long as the rhythm chords--but you should be able to hear this yourself, so no time units are used in writing out whistle effect:

(Holes #3 & #4 with tremolo)

waaaaaah   waaaaaah
   ▼   ▲

waaaaaah   waaaaaah   (back to rhythm)
   ▼   ▲

Try to work this whistle sound into the rhythm smoothly--work on it until it all fits together right. Now let's add another note to the rhythm pattern. Instead of saying "dit/dit" on the draw chord, say "da DIT-dit". The first "dit" is capitalized to indicate that you hit it a little harder or emphasize it a bit more than the others--it's an accent mark.) Now let's substitute this phrase for the draw chord used before and use the same blow chords--it comes out like this:

(Holes #2 & #3)

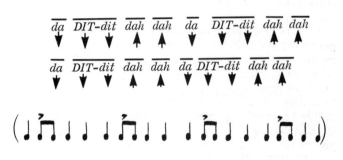

Dig how this changes the rhythm?? (All that's actually happened is that in the original "dit/dit dah/ dah" phrase we've made two notes out of the second "dit"--dig?) This phrase takes the same time to play as the phrase before, but the added note gives it a bit of swing. You'll notice that it sounds better if you don't cut off the blow (dah dah) chords quite as sharply as you do the draw (dit-dit) chords. Don't try to do this too fast at first--get it right slowly, at a speed you can handle, then go faster as you can control it faster. Tommy McClennan (the Mississippi bluesman) used to say, "Take your time boy and play it right!" For right now, control is much more important than speed. Play with this rhythm until you're on top of it.

Now let's get a little fancier and add another little phrase to this rhythm--like spice. The front is the same, you say "da DIT-dit" while drawing in on holes #2 and #3, but here's the difference: for the "dah dah" blow phrase, substitute "hah-a-hah"--blowing out on the first "hah", drawing in on the "a" and blowing out again on the second "hah". This "hah-a-hah" phrase takes the same amount of time to play as the "dah dah" phrase--all we've done is to split the first "dah" into two notes, each half as long as the "dah". It sounds harder than it is. Dig it:

(Holes #2 & #3)

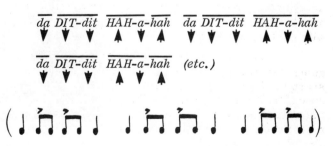

Did you get the timing there? Remember that the "hah-a" is equal to the "dah" used before, and that the final "hah" is also the same time as a "dah" used before. Notice the two accent marks in this phrase-- the first "dit" and the first "hah" are both emphasized slightly. In playing this phrase, it might be easier to think the "hah-a-hah" phrase, rather than actually trying to form it with your mouth...let your breath make the sound through the harp. It's like breathing out-in-out rapidly (pant like you're hot)-- try it without the harp a few times if you have trouble getting it. Work on this pattern until you've got it straight.

Now let's alternate this new phrase with the one used before--like this:

(Holes #2 and #3 again)

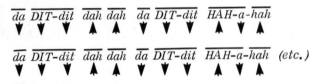

Try using your foot taps to help you get the rhythm. Tap once on the "da dit/dit" phrase, and once on the "dah dah" and alternate "hah-a-hah" phrase. If you can't hack that, tap more often--but that is where the main beats are. Start out slowly again, and speed up only as fast as you can control it. Play this until you've got it down right--it's one of the basic foundations for rhythm accompanying. With this phrase (and the many possible variations on it) you can play behind most any fast blues. The main thing is control--hit the notes cleanly, cut 'em off sharply and keep the accents straight so that you've got a good solid rhythm base.

Now when you play the above in holes #2 and #3 you're playing a tonic chord (for crossed harp)

--if you move up a bit and use holes #4 and #5 it becomes a subdominant chord. So if we add a run for the dominant progression, we'll have a whole standard pattern.

Try this: draw in on hole #1 (which is the dominant note, same as in the hole #4 but one octave down) saying "dah dit/dit/dit dah", repeat it again, then do the same thing blowing out through the #1 hole. Then blow out on hole #2 (holding the note some), blow out on #3 (hold it again)--do it twice more, then draw in on holes #2 and #3, and with your free hand add the tremolo sound. Totally confused?? Here's how it looks:

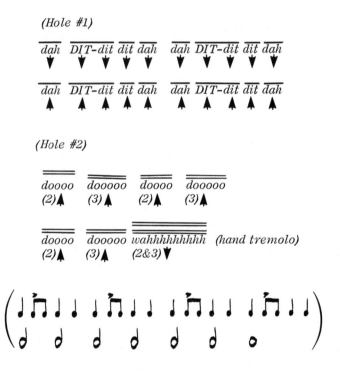

Dig the timing: the "doooo" notes are all two units long, while the "waaaaaah" is four. Work on this till you got it right.

Photo by Frederic Ramsey, Jr.

Now let's put all these various pieces together, and we'll get a standard progression that works out to be just twelve bars long (according to Spider John who counts and spells pretty good).   Try playing the whole thing one time:

(Holes #2 & #3 tonic)

```
 _                _                        _
 da DIT-dit   dah dah   da DIT-dit   HAH-a-hah
 ▼  ▼  ▼      ▲   ▲      ▼  ▼  ▼      ▲   ▼  ▲

 _                _                        _
 da DIT-dit   dah dah   da DIT-dit   HAH-a-hah
 ▼  ▼  ▼      ▲   ▲      ▼  ▼  ▼      ▲   ▼  ▲

 _                _                        _
 da DIT-dit   dah dah   da DIT-dit   HAH-a-hah
 ▼  ▼  ▼      ▲   ▲      ▼  ▼  ▼      ▲   ▼  ▲

 _                _                        _
 da DIT-dit   dah dah   da DIT-dit   HAH-a-hah
 ▼  ▼  ▼      ▲   ▲      ▼  ▼  ▼      ▲   ▼  ▲
```

(Holes #4 & #5 subdominant)

```
 _                _                        _
 da DIT-dit   dah dah   da DIT-dit   HAH-a-hah
 ▼  ▼  ▼      ▲   ▲      ▼  ▼  ▼      ▲   ▼  ▲

 _                _                        _
 da DIT-dit   dah dah   da DIT-dit   HAH-a-hah
 ▼  ▼  ▼      ▲   ▲      ▼  ▼  ▼      ▲   ▼  ▲
```

(Holes #2 & #3 tonic)

```
 _                _                        _
 da DIT-dit   dah dah   da DIT-dit   HAH-a-hah
 ▼  ▼  ▼      ▲   ▲      ▼  ▼  ▼      ▲   ▼  ▲

 _                _                        _
 da DIT-dit   dah dah   da DIT-dit   HAH-a-hah
 ▼  ▼  ▼      ▲   ▲      ▼  ▼  ▼      ▲   ▼  ▲
```

(Hole #1)

dominant
```
 _                                  _
 dah DIT-dit   dit dah   dah DIT-dit-dit dah
 ▼   ▼   ▼     ▼   ▼     ▼   ▼   ▼   ▼   ▼
```

subdominant
```
 _                                  _
 dah DIT-dit   dit dah   dah DIT-dit-dit dah
 ▲   ▲   ▲     ▲   ▲     ▲   ▲   ▲   ▲   ▲
```

(Hole #2)

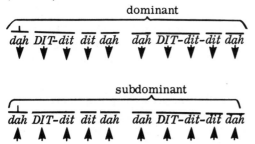

transitional
```
 doooo   doooo   doooo   doooo
 (2)▲    (3)▲    (2)▲    (3)▲
```

tonic
```
 doooo   doooo   wahhhhhhhhh   (hand tremolo)
 (2)▲    (3)▲    (2&3)▼
```

And then you're all set to begin over again. Notice these symbols ___? Each one of those upright marks is the beginning of a bar--count 'em and you get twelve--this is the most standard blues form--12-bar. If you tapped your foot once on the "da dit-dit" and once on the "dah dah" or alternate "hah-a-hah" phrase you were tapping out four beats per bar--which is a good solid rhythm. Work out with this until it comes naturally, so that you can play it without having to read every note. (If you just can't flat play it take it to Western Union and see what they come up with.) This is a good rhythm pattern, but not by any means the only one. But dig how by building from the basic "dit-dit dah-dah" in and out phrase you can put together all kinds of rhythm accompaniments.

For example, in the above pattern you were starting out right on the beat. Let's try "jumping the beat"--coming in a little ahead of it. What happens is that you begin playing on the upbeat (when your foot comes up, getting ready to tap) instead of on the downbeat, which is what you did in the 12-bar pattern. Let's take one of the same phrases from before, only change the time around some--like this:

(Holes #2 & 3)

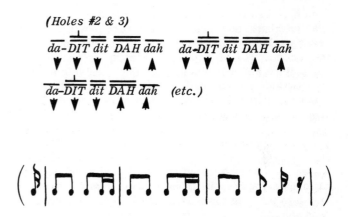

Same basic phrase as before, only the rhythm is changed around some. If you have trouble with the rhythm, say "at-TACK the DOC-tor". Try tapping your feet on the accented (capitalized) notes. See how the "da" comes ahead of the taps?? (Also dig the bar marks--the phrase begins ahead of the bars.) This is a common blues harp technique--to jump the beat some. The alternate "hah-a-hah" phrase comes out like this:

(Holes #2 and #3)

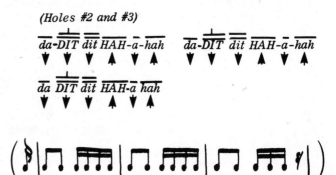

The rhythm here is like saying "at-TACK the DIR-ty dog". Now try putting these phrases in place of the ones used in the last 12-bar pattern. Remember that you begin to play on the upbeat (the beat comes on "TACK"). When you come to the changes (from tonic to subdominant and back again), hold the last "hah" for two time units instead of one--it fits better.

See the possibilities? The above is the same phrase with a different rhythm accent--and there are all kinds of variations possible--see what you can come up with, building from the basic "dit dit dah dah" pattern.

Notice also that in the 12-bar pattern you don't always stick to the basic crossed position of #2 hole in, #4 hole out and #4 hole in--there are several ways to get each chord tone--and they can all be used. In fact, it's a good idea to try different approaches to accompanying the same chord on a guitar. Sometimes it sounds best to run through a dominant pattern way up on the harp in the third octave, sometimes the first and lowest octave works out best--and other times the middle range is best after all--and the same holds true for the other chords. In other words, stay loose and swing with what's happening. Use the basic patterns or positions only as basics--build on them. In blues harp playing, whatever works <u>and</u> <u>fits</u> is right. Don't be afraid to experiment. The only way you'll learn how to play is by playing and experimenting. Once you've got good foundations you can build most any kind of weird structures you want--but without strong foundations they won't stand long.

Try some experiments with tone effects.

Draw in steadily on holes #2 and #3--now alternate your tongue from pointing towards your teeth to pointing towards the roof of your mouth... see what it does to the tone? Try it on the out chord, too.

Also on the out breath, through holes #2 and #3, try making a "brrrrrr"ing noise with your tongue--use the tip of it near the base of your teeth-- pretty much the same way your tongue would vibrate when you tried to sound like a motor as a kid. This isn't an effect you'll want to use frequently, but it's nice to have it when you need it. You can do it on the in breath too--you use the back of your tongue with saliva on it, and sort of gargle, like you were trying to clear the back of your throat. Sounds pretty slimy, but that's how it works.

You've already learned how to get a tremolo sound using your hands--now try the same effect using your breath alone. First try this, without a harp: draw your breath in sharply, like a gasp, towards the back of the roof of your mouth. Hear that "cuk" sound? An anatomy cat I know tells me that it's the epiglottis clicking--and that the epiglottis is a little trapdoor thing which fits over the pipes leading to your lungs. Its main job is to stay shut while you're swallowing food or juice so that nothing bad gets into your lungs. Being as the glot don't really have a lot to do, let's put it to work for harp playing. Have you ever had a foreign language course where you had to use "glottal stops" in pronunciation? I haven't--but I been told that it's about the same as what you do here. The back of your tongue lifts rapidly towards the back of your throat, closing the gap between your tongue and the opening to your throat. Also something weird happens in your throat which I can't explain--but don't fight it (unless you happen to be choking to death). Now try to get a medium fast series of these "stops" all in one breath intake... almost like a controlled spasm, or a deep sobbing. Now do it while drawing on holes #2 and #3 of the harp. If it don't work, try saying "ca-ca-ca-ca". Rather than a series of sharp clicks or stops it should flow and melt together--so that you get a crying or sobbing sound. You may have some trouble with this at first, but it's well worth working on. You notice that this same technique works on the out breath as well, but it's a little harder to control. Try this "throat" tremolo on an in breath then blow out and use your hand for the tremolo. Nice, huh? This is one of the basic sounds of many folk or down-home blues harp styles.

Another way to make a tremolo sound is to use your jaw muscles. With your mouth open just a little, draw in through holes #2 and #3. Now make your teeth chatter, the way they do when you're cold. Dig that you can get a very fast tremolo this way, either on the in or out breath, through once again, it works a lot better on the in breath.

By now you're hip that it takes a lot of wind to make these techniques work—and there ain't any cop-outs here. You just got to get down and work with it. Play with these rhythm chords and tonal effects until you got them all under control. And then we can get down to the meat of it--bending notes.

8

"Bending" Notes

First off, why is it necessary to "bend" notes? Well, we all have to have our little perversions, right?

Two reasons: the physical construction of the harp, and the African-influenced "blues tonality." A blues singer generally goes along with the standard diatonic scale, according to European tonality, except in two places. The third and seventh notes of the scale are generally sung a little bit flat, according to the European-trained ear. These are called "blue notes"---they derive from the traditional African tonality and they are what gives the blues its distinctive sound.

(For a detailed study see THE STORY OF JAZZ by Marshall Stearns--pgs. 195-200--see Kidney II.)

The other reason is that two notes of the scale (fa and la, whatever the key) are omitted in the first octave of the harp--and sometimes you need those notes. The only way to get them is to make them by "bending" the sound of the next reed above flat--so that it produces a tone lower in pitch than the one it was designed to produce, and closer to the note you need. You can make a note flat by bending the reed, but you can't make it sharp.

I got told by a physics cat that what happens when you bend a note is like this: When you play a harp in the usual fashion you have one "resonance system" in operation--the air column vibrates both in the harp and in the mouth cavity, causing the reed to vibrate at its normal pitch. When you "bend" a note (make it flat) you change the shape of your mouth, position of your tongue etc. and you put another resonance system into operation--which changes the pitch. I'm not quite sure I understand all that, but I know that it works, and that's all that matters anyway.

First, you have to be able to produce a clear single tone by narrowing your lips leaving your tongue free. If you can't, you're going too fast--go back a ways (do not pass "go", do not collect $200) and take it a little slower.

Now draw in on the second hole, fairly hard. Notice how your tongue is in "neutral", just sort of cooling it there in the middle of your mouth? And dig how the air drawn in through the harp passes back in a straight line, over the tongue, towards the back of your throat.

Try this now: sing down the scale as low as you can go...then try to go farther. Notice how your lower jaw drops down a little and tenses? And how the whole front of your tongue drops to the bottom of your mouth cavity? Hold your lowest forced note and bring your tongue back to "neutral"--raises the pitch a little, don't it? So you see, dropping your tongue helps out some in lowering the pitch.

And this is pretty much what you do when you bend notes--you try to force or bend the column of air drawn in thru the harp down. Try it: draw in on the #2 hole. Now tense your jaw a little and drop it some, bring your tongue down to the bottom of the front of your mouth, and at the same time try to suck the air through the harp towards the tip of your tongue. It also helps to narrow down the size of your lip opening--pucker up, mother! It takes a lot of wind to do this--you need about twice the pressure to bend a note to get the same volume as when not bending. Dig that the tip of your tongue curls <u>back</u> and down--not just down.

Any luck? If you didn't get it the first time, try again. And keep on trying--it may damn near drive you nuts--but the first time it works you'll wonder why it was such a hassle--'cause it's so easy once you get it. Some people can do it the first time-- others take a long time to get it. The main thing is not to give up in disgust. If it doesn't come after a reasonable amount of work, go back and fool with some rhythm patterns or tone techniques for awhile, then come on back and try again. I had a hassle picking it up at first, but when I finally made it I was one satisfied cat.

There is another way to bend notes, but it's sort of a cop-out and it's not half as flexible as the technique above. What you do is just pivot the harp, using your lips as the pivot point. Try pivoting the front (sounding side) of the harp up, so that the holes are almost pointing down into your lower lip, and at the same time suck the air in harder. Now you can probably get a bend a little easier this way, but it's a sloppier technique, and harder to work with in the long run. As of matter of fact, I'd use it only as a last resort.

If you've been getting your single notes by tongue blocking, try bending by just letting the edge of your tongue slip over and partially cover the open hole--and draw harder at the same time. The bend takes place in only a very small movement of your tongue. Practice and you'll get so that you can control it--go too far and you kill it altogether. If you want to play chromatic harp in blues style it'd be best to work a lot on bending notes this way.

However you do it (for most styles I prefer and recommend the first method), work on getting a clean unwavering note--so that it stays bent and doesn't quiver back and forth. Here's a little exercise for you. Go through the first holes in sequence-- in first position like this:

1▲ 1▼ 2▲ 2▼ 3▼ 4▲

Hear where the missing notes in the scale are? Now go through it again, but this time try putting in the missing notes by bending the reed next above down to the right pitch--like this:

1▲ 1▼ 2▲ 2↘ 2▼ 3↘ 3▼ 4▲
                B   B

Your bent tones are the #2 and #3 holes in--shown above by the bent arrows and the letter "B" (clever, eh?). If you can't hear the exact pitch of the missing notes get somebody to play the scale on a guitar or piano (or zither, or gourd, or sitar, or--). Remember that this exercise is in first position, so the scale would be in the same key that the harp is tuned in. Don't get hung up if you can't get exactly the right pitch notes at first--it'll come in time. But try to get as close as possible--so that it sounds like a complete scale.

After you've made a reasonable fascimile of a scale try this: start out drawing in on the #2 hole, bending the tone to make the missing note of the scale (D on an A harp, F on a C harp and so on-- it's the fourth note of the scale). Then instead of making a sharp jump to your next note (which is drawn in the same hole, but without bending), try sliding up to it slowly. What happens is that your tongue slowly slides up towards the harp from the bottom of your mouth, raising the tone as it comes. You'll notice that the closer in pitch the reed gets to the tone it was built to make, the louder it'll become--so you gradually have to decrease the air pressure as you slide up. Now try sliding up to the actual pitch of the bent note—but when you almost reach the actual pitch widen your lips so that you get both holes #2 and #3 (a tonic chord in cross-harp playing) and at the same time get a tremolo sound by vibrating your free hand in front of the harp. Groovy, ain't it?

Now, try bending notes in the other holes. The higher you go, the harder the notes get to bend-- right? That's because as the pitch gets higher, the reeds get shorter--and the shorter they are, the harder they are to work with. Also it takes less tongue movement on the higher reeds to produce the

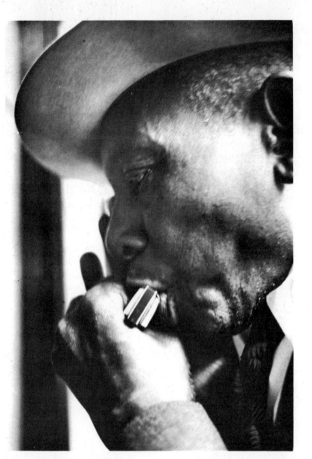

Jazz Gillum   Photo by Raeburn Flerlage

same amount of bend as on the low ones, and the less movement needed, the harder it is to control. So for all practical purposes, you'd best forget about bending any draw notes above the #7 hole.

Dig that I said <u>draw</u> notes--blow notes are much easier to bend on the higher reeds than on the lower ones. Bending blow notes requires a little different technique. Try blowing out thru the #7 hole, with a lot of pressure. Now purse your lips and narrow them down, increasing the pressure. And this time instead of dropping down your tongue should tighten up some and move a fraction towards your teeth. Any luck?? This will work on most of the higher notes—on the lower ones it won't, since the lower reeds are longer and take a lot more wind than most people have to force them flat. So for bends on the lower blow notes, the tongue method is best. (Same as before--the edge of the tongue partially covers the hole you're playing.) Try this and you'll see that draw notes are much easier to bend and control, even though blow bends are possible and sometimes necessary.

But the draw (or in) bends are most important in most blues harp styles--in cross position, your "blue" transition notes are on draw tones. For example, say you're doing a chord rhythm in the tonic (draw, holes #2 and #3) and you're ready to change to the subdominant. Here's a nice way to get

into it: go up to the #4 hole and draw, and, while still drawing, bend the tone down as far as you can go-- when you reach the limit of the bend, switch quickly to blow in the same hole--and at the same time open your lips so that you get a blow chord on holes #4 and #5. This should be a fluid phrase--a slur of notes run together rather than three separate notes. Starting out with the tonic chord it looks like this:

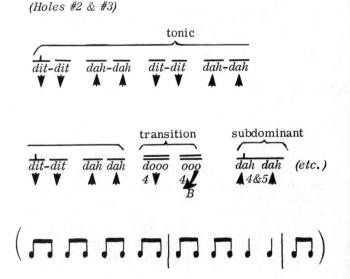

The first subdominant chord comes right after the transitional bend, snapping at its heels. Now let's put in a subdominant phrase with a transitional bend back to the tonic. It's different--draw in on the #3 hole, bend it down as far as you can, then open up your lips and draw on holes #2 and #3--which is the tonic chord again. Like before, this should be fluid, like a continuous flow of notes, rather than separate tones following after each other. (The difference between this and the other transitional bend is that instead of going to a blow note after the bend, you stay on the draw note, opening to a chord.) Here's the whole subdominant phrase with the transition to the tonic at the end:

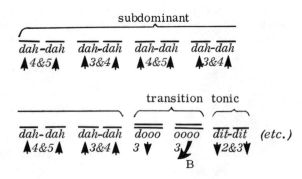

Notice that this is all on the out breath and it'll take a big set of lungs to make it all on one breath (do blondes really have an advantage?)--or a quick pause for breath. Again, the tonic comes right after the transition, right on its heels, as a continuous smear of notes.

Now you stay in the tonic and chord along until time to change to the dominant. Let's get fancy and use a dominant single note run instead of just a chord. Try this--draw in on the #3 hole, blow on the #4, draw on the #4, and in on the #4 once more, bending it this time--then out on the 3rd. Works like this:

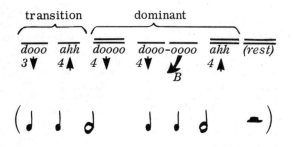

Get the timing?? "Rest" means just that--cool it for two time units before the next phrase begins. Dig that the first part of this phrase actually belongs to the tonic progression.

Now let's add a resolving subdominant phrase with another transitional bend back to the

tonic. Try to play it from the diagram:

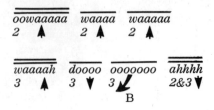

Dig the timing there. Feel kind of up tight about this phrase? Doesn't it sort of leave you hanging? Let's add some chords that finish it off (they switch back and forth from tonic to dominant) and end with a simple run on the dominant--which fills out the pattern nicely and leaves you all set to begin again on the tonic. Like this:

(Holes #2 & #3)

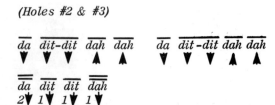

You recognize the first part of that from before, right? Get the timing straight on the ending--it's a frequently-used one in many bluesharp styles. Now let's put all of these pieces together and have an orgy in sound, filling in the tonic phrase to make a complete pattern. Try playing it through one time:

(Holes #2 & #3 Tonic)

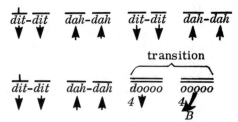

(Subdominant)

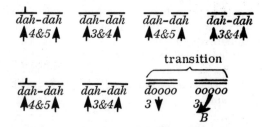

(Holes #2 and #3 tonic)

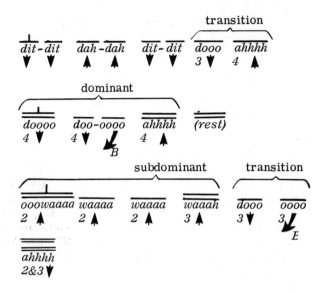

transition

<u>dit</u>-<u>dit</u> <u>dah</u>-<u>dah</u> <u>dit</u>-<u>dit</u> <u>dooo</u> <u>ahhhh</u>
▼ ▼   ▲ ▲   ▼ ▼   3 ▼   4 ▲

dominant

<u>doooo</u> <u>doo-oooo</u> <u>ahhhh</u>   (rest)
4 ▼   4 ▼ ↙B   4 ▲

subdominant   transition

<u>ooowaaaa</u> <u>waaaa</u> <u>waaaa</u> <u>waaah</u> <u>dooo</u> <u>oooo</u>
2 ▲   2 ▲   2 ▲   3 ▲   3 ▼ 3 ↙E

<u>ahhhh</u>
2&3 ▼

(Holes #2 and #3)

<u>da</u> <u>dit</u>-<u>dit</u> <u>dah</u> <u>dah</u>   <u>da</u> <u>dit</u>-<u>dit</u> <u>dah</u> <u>dah</u>
▼   ▼ ▼   ▲   ▲   ▼   ▼ ▼   ▲   ▲

<u>da</u> <u>dit</u> <u>dit</u> <u>dah</u> (rest)
2▼ 1▼ 1▼ 1▼

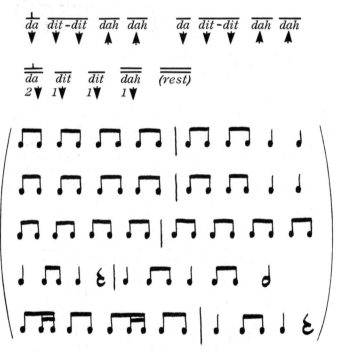

And there you jolly well are, ready to start the pattern from the front again. Spider John (who counts and spells pretty good) says that this is actually a

10-bar blues--(dig the marks above the notes, like before) which shows you how you can play around with the form some and still have it work out okay. (If you absolutely going to wig out if it ain't a straight 12-bar, just add two more bars to the first tonic section.)

Whichever way you do, go through this a few times in sucession. Get the bends working in smooth and right, without wavers or hassles--get confident, in other words. And when you've got this down pat (or Mary or pick one), go back to the last complete pattern diagrammed and go through it one time--only use some transitional bends on the changes.

And right now would be a good time to go back to the front of this crossed-harp section and review the whole thing.

Then put the book away for awhile and see what you can come up with by yourself. Dig records--listen for transitions, bent notes, tremolos, phrasing, rhythm patterns and so on...in other words quit sweating and ball some. But a word here first--before you get to feeling too cocky--I know a cat who can get four separate clear and distinct notes from the first hole of a G harp, draw. (Try it, if you think it's easy.) When you can do that, <u>then</u> pound on your chest and signify. In the meantime, ball with what you know and get to know what you know well. Work towards getting everything tight, clean, and under control--so that the harp follows your head, instead of you chasing after it. Make it work for and with you.

This pretty well covers the basics of second position or crossed harp--you'll find some more specific playing techniques farther on, but you got the foundation here. I'm not going to come on and say that this is all there is to know--I'm still learning myself and I guess probably everybody is--but this is most of what I know. If you can find better ways to make things work, fine, groove with them.

Cross harp will carry you through most blues harp styles, but third and fourth positions are worth knowing about--so read through their sections anyhow--there are some other effects there you might have use for.

The Genuine Joseph Emmett Richter

Furry Lewis, Gus Cannon and Memphis Willie B.

Photo by David Gahr

9

Third Position

As you've dug, a "position" in blues harp refers to the key you play it in--or, where you find your starting (tonic) note. In straight, or first, position the tonic note is #1 hole blow, in crossed or second position your tonic is #2 hole draw--theoretically, there are as many positions as there are notes on a harp--but it doesn't work out in practice. (In some positions you can't get chords, in others the main tones are all bend notes, sometimes the transitional notes are blow rather than draw and as a result harder to bend for "blue tonality".) So for all practical purposes there are only four main positions. The most often used is crossed, or second position, but the other two have several useful advantages. Dig third position.

In second position you play a harp tuned a fourth above the guitar key, in the same key as the guitar, right? The "same key" part holds true for both third and fourth positions--you always play harp in the same key as the guitar--no matter what key the harp is tuned to.

In third position you play a harp tuned only one tone (two steps) below the guitar key. Turn back to the chromatic scale at the beginning of the crossed harp section. Third position is two steps down on this scale. Say the guitar is in E--you count down (to the left) two steps (or halftones), beginning with the tone next to E (D#) and you end on D--which is the harp used to play third position accompaniment to a guitar playing in E. With the guitar in G count down two and you get F--and so on...until you come to a guitar in F. If you count down two you land on a D# harp tuning--and you don't find them around. So the only way to get around this is to have the guitar man capo up one fret, so that F fingering positions come out with an actual pitch of F#. Then when you count down two, you land on an E harp, so you're straight. However, there ain't too many guitar men around who play that much in F, so its nickle-dime anyhow. Here are the main tone holes:

THIRD POSITION

tonic	subdominant	dominant
4 ▼	3 ▲	6 ▼

Notice that third position follows the same pattern as second: both the tonic and dominant are draw notes, and the subdominant is a blow note. Dig this simple blues in D:

(D-tonic)
Did you ever dream lucky, wake up achin' in mind?

  (G-subdominant)   (D)
Did you ever dream lucky, wake up achin' in mind?

(A-dominant)   (G)   (D)
And you know you're losin' more'n you'll ever find.

      Now to accompany in third position, use a C harp and play it in D (at the basic simplest) like this:

1st line: Draw #4 hole (D).
2nd line: Blow #3 hole (G) and Draw #4 hole (D).
3rd line: Draw #6 hole (A), Blow #3 hole (G) and Draw #4 hole (D).

Remember that on a C harp there are two G notes available--either as a blow or draw note (the same is true for other keys as well--two ways to get the subdominant tone)--it's used as a blow note here because the other two chords are draw--and if all three were draw you'd have a breathing problem--sucking all that air in without ever getting rid of any can get painful. Dig that you have to use mostly single notes--if you open up two holes you get discords--but ty this:

      Take hold of the harp with your free hand with the thumb beneath and the index finger on top.

Now draw in on holes #4 and #5 and move the harp rapidly back and forth, parallel to your lips. You should get a definite warbling sound. You don't have to move the harp far, and your lips should follow the movement slightly (keep 'em loose) so that only holes #4 and #5 sound. Now if you play this with the tonic chord on a guitar it sounds like a discord that isn't a discord--it's sort of a compromise between the two notes. The faster you move the harp, the faster the warble. (This warble works in cross position too... try it on the transitions from tonic to subdominant chords in the diagrammed patterns.) This is a groovy effect that comes in handy in all positions, but especially in third. This warble is one of the basic trademarks of "Chicago" style harp--the R&B sound of people like Little Walter and Junior Wells. This semi-discord adds greatly to the R&B sound--it has an eerie driving effect when amplified and builds up a lot of excitement.

      Jimmy Reed (and other harp men who work with single notes a lot) also sometimes use third position--since, using it you can now get three keys from each harp (which is handy if you're broke or keep losing harps), play a D harp in first position you can accompany guitar in D, play it in second position and you can accompany the key of A, play it in third and you can accompany E.

      There are disadvantages to third position, though--you can't do too much chording for rhythm accompaniment. (Unless you use the subdominant as a draw tone--then you can chord using holes #2 and #3--but if you're playing steadily, without many pauses in a number, you'll have a breathing problem.) For that reason you'll find little (if any) folk-style harp in third--it's most all in cross position, which comes easier and more naturally to most people. (There's more on third position in the section on Sonny Boy Williamson--diagrammed out.) For now just work out with a guitar man or records. Try playing any 12-bar blues in third position. Use the warble effect on the tonic--and try it while drawing in on the subdominant.

      There aren't any diagrams here because by this point you should be starting to work things out for yourself. The same basics apply here as in second position: get clean notes, hit them true, and get used to finding the right tones without having to count up to them. In short, get it under control. And the only way to do that is to work out with it. A guitar cat will help a lot since it's hard to hear the changes if you're working solo. If you're really interested in third position, check out the list of sides at the back of the books, and dig some of the R&B ones-- you can hear more in one listening then I can tell you in 20 pages.

10

Fourth Position

Fourth is still another key to play the same harp in. I discovered it (I'm not saying I was the first cat to find out about it, but I discovered it for myself) one night when I was trying to find out what key harp was on a certain record. The band was in G#--but there was a harp playing it, in tune-- and it didn't sound like a chromatic. None of the other three positions have anything about playing with G# in them--so I figured there must be another one. After experimenting a while I found there was-- fourth position. After I found the right harp for G# I went to work on figuring out how it worked and why. Twelve hours later, bleary-eyed and raving insane, I'd figured, crosschecked, multiplied and subtracted myself into a stupor--but I figured it out. And here's how it works.

You're still playing in the same key as the accompaniment--in this case you use a harp that's tuned a third below the key of the guitar. Check out the chromatic scale back there (pg. 23) again. Fourth position is four steps (or halftones) down on this scale. Say the guitar's in E--count down four (starting with D#) and you land on C--which is the harp used to play fourth position accompaniment with guitar in E. Or take A--count down (to the left) four and you get F...and so on. If you go through all keys you'll see that three keys aren't available--C, F and G (count down from C and you'll see why)--but you can accompany guitar with an actual pitch of C#, F# and G# if the guitar has a capo on the first fret.

Here's a blues in E:

(E tonic)
Rock me baby, honey with a steady roll,
   (A-subdominant)   (E)
Yes rock me baby, child with a steady roll,

(B 7th--dominant   (A)   (E)
Rock me right, if you wanna save you goddam soul.

To accompany this in fourth position, use a C harp like this:

1st line: Blow #2 hole (E)
2nd line: Draw #6 hole (A) and Blow #2 hole (E)
3rd line: Draw #3 hole (B), Draw #6 hole
     (A) and Blow #2 hole (E)

Or the other way, it looks like this:

FOURTH POSITION

tonic	subdominant	dominant
2 ▲	6 ▼	3 ▼

Dig the difference between this and second and third positions--you still have two draw notes and one blow--but the draw notes fall on the subdominant and dominant instead of tonic and dominant chords.

The above is only a skeleton of the form-- in actual practice it gets added to, and often changed. With somebody playing a tonic chord on a guitar, try this: blow out through the #3 hole twice, then out through the #2 once, like this:

dooooo   *doooooo*   *waaaaah*
 3 ▲   *3* ▲   *2* ▲

Hit the notes on the #3 hole cleanly, but put a bend and quiver on the note in the #2 hole and hold it twice as long as either of the first notes. Or, while still

on the tonic chord, open up holes #2 and #3, blow and use your free hand to vibrate the harp for the warbling sound--weird, ain't it??

Now on the subdominant chord of the guitar, instead of drawing in on the #6 hole, try blowing through the #4 and #5--adding the warble with your hand again. Somehow or other it works.

And on the dominant, instead of just drawing in on the #3 hole, open it up and get the #4 as well--again with the warble. Works pretty well, eh?? So you see that you don't always have to stick to the basic position--you can screw it around some, just so long as it works.

You probably have figured out by now that this is another good "Chicago" position-- and it's also good for slow, ominous kinds of blues...the tones have a weird sound to them--it sounds almost modal.

There are disadvantages in fourth as well, though, melodies are a little harder to work in, as is blues tonality--but fourth is a good compromise between cross and third position harp: since you can play both a bit of melody and rhythm--just as long as you return to the basic notes somewhere in the chord progression.

Try fourth position--either with a guitar cat or with records. Although you probably won't use either fourth or third much, they're good to know--maybe you'll only need them on one number, but on that one number they'll be the only way to make it. Besides, what the hell--it never hurts to know more than you need to use--then you can sit around and look smug.

Try fourth position as amplified harp--it's a boss kick. Fourth is also good for playing a Marine Band with records where chromatics were used and the accompaniment is in a sharped key... see what other uses you can find for it. But keep it clean.

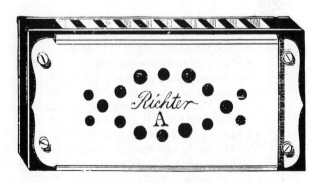

11 Chromatic Harmonicas

Generally speaking chromatic harps aren't much use for blues. They have the disadvantages of stiffer reeds which are harder to bend (they tend to "flat out" as soon as the bend begins), they're more complicated and harder to handle, and the tone layout makes chord accompaniment difficult.

The only style where they're used to much advantage at all is Chicago R&B. Here they have the advantage of a full organ-like tone when amplified (the Marine Band usually sounds a little shriller), they can be played in any key (within reason), and the tone layout makes them a good lead instrument. There are many recorded instrumentals where the lead is played with a chromatic harp.

Remember the differences between the diatonic and chromatic scales? (Diatonic is eight tones, one octave on the white keys of a piano, Chromatic is twelve tones, an octave using both black and white piano keys.) All that a chromatic harp is is two diatonic harps, tuned one half step apart, placed one above the other. The drawing below shows a Hohner Chromonica 260.

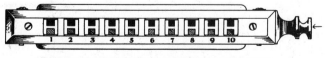

This shows a full view of the Chromonica mouthpiece. Arrow points to the lever.

Figure 6

Say that this one is tuned in C. (They come in C or G.) The harp on top is tuned diatonically in C, the harp on the bottom is tuned diatonically in C#. When the lever is in the normal position, (out, as above) (it's held out by a spring), the holes of the top or C are exposed, while the bottom or C# harp holes are closed off by the slide lever. When you push the button in, the reverse happens: the C harp is closed off, and the C# harp is opened up. With this setup it is possible to get all twelve tones--the natural notes on the C harp, the sharps and flats on the C# harp-- all you have to do is press the button and move the slide. Dig the drawing below.

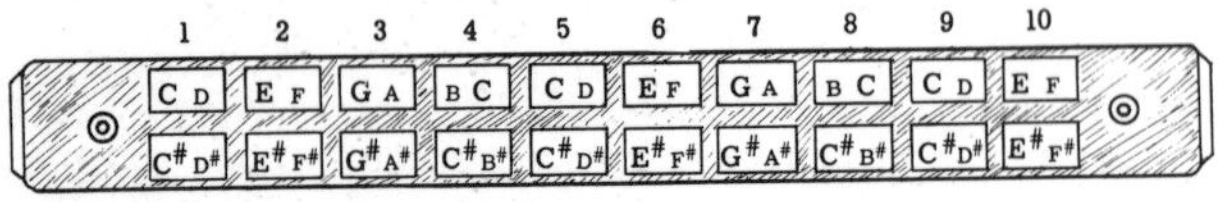

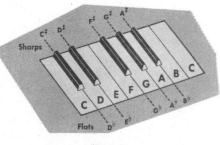

Figure 7

The top row of notes are for the C harp (in other words when the slide is in normal, or out position), the bottom row for the C# harp--when the slide is pushed in. In both cases, the big letters are blow, the small are draw. Try a chromatic scale one time. Blow in the #1 hole, with the slide out. Push the slide in, blow in the same hole and you get a tone one half-step up. Release the slide and draw on the same hole, you get a tone another half-step up. Push the slide in, draw (still on the same hole), and you get a tone still another half step up in pitch....and so forth for each hole. BUT--notice the repeated tones? (#2 hole blow, with the slide in, is the same as #2 hole draw, with the slide out--and #4 hole draw, slide in, is the same as #4 hole blow, with the slide out.) But if you check the above diagram you see that there aren't any tones repeated--somebody goofed, huh??? HOO-HAH—you forgot something: on the chromatic scale there aren't any such tones as B# and E#. Dig the drawing of a keyboard below.

Figure 8

Dig that there are no black keys between B and C and E and F--so B# is actually C and E# is actually F...which is what they are in this harp. So the note marked B# in the tone layout is actually C--why call it B#?? Damned if I know..that's how they did it-- and until the revolution we're stuck with it.) Notice that in the #4 and #8 holes the lower tone (B) is a

draw note and the higher tone (C) is a blow note--and that the C note is repeated as a blow note in the next hole. This is so that each scale begins with C as a blow note and D as a draw note in the same hole.

Rather than waste the time by going into a long detailed study of playing chromatic harp, let's just stick to the chromatic as it is used in blues. (If you're interested in other styles, or want to learn more about the basics, try these books: THE PLEASURE OF MUSIC WITH YOUR HOHNER CHROMATIC ($ .75) or QUICK SUCCESS METHOD ($3.95), both available from music stores or direct from M. Hohner, Inc.

The same relationship applies here as with the Marine Bands--you always play in the same key as the accompaniment, generally following along with the tonic-subdominant-dominant progression. But on a chromatic harp, each key starts in a different position (i.e. the tonic note for the key of D is #4 hole draw, slide out, for C# the tonic note is #5 hole draw, slide in---etc.). Also remember that in the Marine Bands the sharps and flats necessary for the key are built in--on a chromatic you have to put them in yourself...so a knowledge of music helps here...but it ain't necessary. (The "Sharps in Harps" table in the reference section might be of some help if you really want to work at it--it gives the sharps and/or flats for each key.)

Probably blues have been played in all keys on chromatics, but the ones that show up most frequently are D, G, G#, C and sometimes B-flat-- and the most frequent one is D#.

Rather than go through horrendously long and complicated bunch of diagrams (which'd probably do us both in) I'll just say you're better off to work it out yourself. You can hear and understand things from records which would take pages and pages to explain here...and I'm not sure I could put it in writing anyhow. And remember, none of the harpmen you hear on records have learned from books--they picked it up by themselves.

Actually the only way to learn blues on a chromatic is by playing--play along with records-- dig the phrasing, the runs, the chords used...and then apply what you hear to your own scenes. Learn to listen and listen to learn.

Try this method of learning from records, determine what key the backing is in (use a piano or guitar--they're easier to hear first than harp), then check with the tone diagram above and find the easiest tonic, subdominant and dominant tones--and then work out from there, playing along with the record. Check out the section on Little Walter too.

So much for 'words to live by.'

42

12 A Taste of Harp Styles

Blues guitar and vocal styles often tend to get labeled with the names of places they came from-- you get,styles known as "delta" and "Texas" blues-- but in the case of blues harp, where the styles are so highly personal, rather than being regionally identified they're usually labeled with the name of the man who used them best. So in this section you'll find five harpmen who cover a pretty complete span of techniques and times--from the farming south in the thirties to the steel mill north of the fifties.

Rather than try to show how to sound exactly like anyone of these men (which would take five separate books and more patience than I got) I'll skim over the basics of each of their different styles, giving you the beginnings from which you should be able to work by yourself.

By now, you've probably made up your mind which one of the branches of the blues you want to mainly follow, so as a starter I'd suggest using the section covering the man who comes closest to your aims and then go on from there. But remember, you won't learn it all from a book--you got to be listening and playing.

Sonny Terry

Sonny is the boss of country or "folk" blues harp. His fantastic rhythm patterns, falsetto whoops and beautifully controlled runs put him right at the

Sonny Terry   Photo by David Gahr

top of his field. At first hearing most of his recordings sound incredibly complicated, and it's awfully
tempting just to sit back and forget the whole thing.
But his style is based on many of the things you've
already learned, and it can be broken down and
understood.

   Sonny has two separate styles--one when
he's playing solo or lead, and another when he's accompanying. Let's take the solo work first.

   For reference, we'll use one of his earliest solo recordings; HARMONICA AND VOCAL
SOLOS (Folkways 10" LP FA2035). This album is
about equally divided between instrumentals and vocals, and it's worth having, even if you only plan to
listen.

   First, just sit down and listen one time,
all the way through, without a harp. Dig that most of
the effects you've already learned--now all you have
to do is put them together. Notice how he stretches
the blues form to fit his style. He doesn't always
stay in a strict 12-bar form with its tonic-subdomi-

nant-dominant progressions--but all his variations
are built from this form, and usually return to it
when they stray away. Notice the varying ways that
he accompanies a vocal: on BAD LUCK BLUES the
harp is used mostly as chord punctuation through the
verses; on FINE AND FALSE VOICE (RED RIVER) it
alternates with the vocal, sometimes finishing off a
line in place of the voice; on BEAUTIFUL CITY the
harp works in a definite call-and-response pattern
with the vocal, taking the lead on the chorus sometimes; and on WOMEN'S BLUES the harp comments
on the vocal with its own melody lines.

   According to my phonograph, Sonny is
using a Marine Band B-flat harp all the way through
this LP. (This is a good point by the way--most
turntables vary slightly in speed from each other...
and by the time a record goes through all the necessary duplications to get it onto wax the pitch may be
slightly higher or lower than what was originally recorded. So a variable speed machine is a big help in
learning from records--you can correct any pitch
difference with the flick of an ankle.) Sonny holds
his harp upside down (with the low notes to the right)

44

in his right hand and uses his left for cupping. But it's the same as holding it in your left hand, with the low notes to the left--either way you still get a complete cup where it's needed--on the low notes...so don't sweat it.

Let's take apart a few cuts.

ALCOHOLIC BLUES--B-flat, cross position. Notice that the main part of the theme is in the tonic and subdominant progressions, and that the dominant is more suggested than actually played out. Here's a rough transcription in arrow form...just bear in mind that these diagrams are playable approximations and not always a literal note-for-note transcription--in practice, both the rhythm and melodies are a good deal more complex.

(Tonic)

uh   huh   eeee   (hold)
3▼   4▲   4▼

uh   huh   eeee   (hold)
3▼   4▲   4▼

uh   huh   eee   haah
3▼   4▲   4▼   5&6▲

slurred together
waaah   ah   ooo   ooooo   (hold)
4 ▼   3 ▼   2 ▼   2↘B

(Subdominant)

do   ah   do   ah   (hold)   do   ah   do   ah   (hold)
3↘B 3▲ 3↘B 3▲   3↘B 3▲ 3↘B 3▲

daah   daah   di   da-dah   ooooo   (hand tremolo & hold)
4&5▲ 4&5▲ 5▼ 5▲3▼   2&3▼

This whole phrase is repeated, then another tonic-subdominant phrase up around the #6 and #7 holes, back through the tonic part of the above phrase again, finally resolving with subdominant and dominant phrases (with falsetto "whoops" alternating with the harp), a series of cut-off chords for rhythm, and back through the main theme again.

This reads harder than it plays. Try the above phrase a few times slowly, just with the book-- work on the fast slur at the end of the tonic and on the run and the end of the subdominant. Then go through it with the record. If you find that it's too fast at first and you've got a four-speed machine, turn it down to 16 rpm--this'll cut the speed in half and drop the tone almost exactly an octave--so that you can still play along with it. Work with this until you come pretty close to his phrasing and timing.

BAD LUCK BLUES--Also B-flat harp, second position. The opening phrase (or one very much like it) is a favorite of Sonny's and he uses this basic run often. It corresponds to the introductory runs guitarists make before starting on the first verse of a song. Here's a transcription:

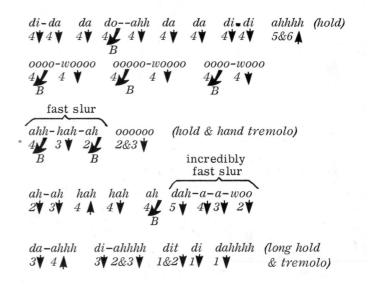

Writing phrases out this way can get to be somewhat confusing. The notes in the brackets should come very fast--almost as one note rather than a series. The notes in the second bracket should completely blend together--it'll help if you move the harp with your free hand to get a slight warble effect. Try this phrase slowly a few times from the book, then try it with the record. And if you think you got a problem reading it--you shoulda seen the hassle I went through writing it out. Dig that in this number Sonny sticks pretty close to the tonic-subdominant-dominant form, and that it's pretty close to a 12-bar form all the way through. Notice the instrumental break (after the second verse)--it's typical of Sonny's style; dig especially the nice double-timing he gets by using cut-off chords--used here as a transition from the tonic to subdominant progression. Try playing along with the record all the way through, following as closely as you can. (The "whoops" are optional.)

SHORTENING BREAD--B-flat harp again--but this time in first position. The whole thing is based on one simple little phrase, repeated over and over with variations. It looks tricky at first, but play easily once you get the rhythm straight...most of this number is in the rhythm anyway. Here's how it goes:

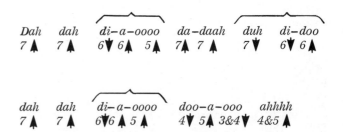

And the rest is all based on this. (The high note later on is #9 hole blow.) Notice that Sonny uses the cup effect for rhythm as well as for tremolo, moving his whole hand in and out, in rhythm. This is one song you can't stay hung-up while you're playing it...you got to feel good to groove with its bouncy little rhythm. The notes in the brackets are rapid-fire again--but try to keep single tones clear. Work on this awhile.

Rather than take all the other songs apart, a few comments on the rest of them: WOMEN'S BLUES comes out to a pitch of about B-flat half-sharpened on my phonograph, so it's kind of hard to play with. LOCOMOTIVE BLUES is in first position, and a large part of the rhythm comes from the tongue moving in the mouth as if to form words, while the hands open and close the cup in rhythm. LOST JOHN is a good one to practice whooping melodies and rhythms on. Notice how the whoops both keep time and fit in logically with the melodic phrases? They're not there just for the hell of it--they carry the song along. FINE AND FALSE voice is good for falsetto singing--also dig the phrasing, and the way his harp and voice interweave, never fighting, but always complementing each other. HARMONICA STOMP is a groovy instrumental to work out with--dig particularly how the sharply cut-off chords and pauses between phrases carry the rhythm along. Sonny is cutting off the chords with his tongue, and at the same time bringing his free hand rapidly towards the harp, closing the cup sharply, which adds to the percussive effect. Try that. BEAUTIFUL CITY is good for getting straight with a call-and-response pattern.

To sum up this Readers-Digest version of Sonny's solo style: He uses his harp for both melody and rhythm--often at the same time. The tremolo effect is used very sparingly, making it all the more effective. The most striking aspects are his use of cut-off chords for rhythm, his single note melodic runs (which either continue the melody, substituting for the vocal, or play counterpoint to it) and the harp-vocal interweaving.

Sonny's style as a sideman is a little different. On the recordings with Leadbelly (see Kidney III) he divides himself pretty evenly between two main accompaniment styles. One is a "follow" style, where the harp sings a mostly single note duet to the melody through the verses, with cut-off chords used as rhythmic punctuation. (Dig ON A MONDAY on the Folkways LP listed in back.) The other style can best be described as "counterpoint"--but both melodically and rhythmically--Sonny uses a series of melodic runs, playing around the melody, with a heavy chord rhythm accompaniment all the way through. (Dig JOHN HENRY on the Stinson LP listed in Kidney III.)

With Woody Guthrie, Sonny played mostly in the follow style, a style made necessary by the type of music that Woody most often played. (Here's a generalization for you: country, country-western and folk harp accompaniment is usually mostly melodic, while blues uses counterpoint harmony and/or

rhythm.) See the listings in back for recording of Sonny with Woody. They're worth having--if only for listening.

Sonny's style of playing with his current partner, Brownie McGhee, is sort of a refinement of techniques used before. On many of their numbers Sonny sings vocal harmony, so his harp just chords between lines, or does short melodic runs, returning to the basic melody line in time for the next line or verse. In most of these duets his main harp work happens in the instrumental choruses; he may follow the melody, play counterpoint to it, chord around it, or mix all three of these together--depending on the needs of the particular number. When Brownie does a solo vocal, Sonny's harp is more complex--he plays little counterpoint runs between lines of the lyrics, and wraps up his variations with a return to the main melody at the end of a verse.

A good record to work with here is BROWNIE McGHEE & SONNY TERRY SING (Folkways FS 2327). First just listen to it all the way through. Notice the familiar patterns that keep showing up? Almost all harpmen use the same basic foundations--it's the emphasis they place on certain effects or techniques that makes their style their own. Dig also that Sonny never uses effects just to show off his technique--they're there because they carry the mood of the song along. (For example-- the explosive passage in the high note range on JOHN HENRY works in tremendously well here--but if it was used often, you'd soon be sick of it.) Notice that Sonny uses the end rhythm pattern from the intro to BAD LUCK BLUES (in on the #1 & #2 hole three times) as a sort of sum-up pattern at the end of verses on the final dominant chord, so that he's set to start the next verse. Notice that he occasionally uses the second octave in holes #4-#7 for variation. Here are the tunings on this LP (according to a borrowed machine):

SIDE ONE		SIDE TWO	
1) A	4) A	1) A	5) F
2) G	5) A	2) A	6) B-flat
3) A	6) A	3) D	7) A
		4) A	

The keys listed are harp keys, so you're all set. They are all in second or cross position--try playing along with the record one time. Don't worry if you can't make the exact notes the first time--just get used to Sonny's phrasing and timing habits--later on you can concentrate on narrowing in on the exact phrases used. Remember that almost all bends and cut-off chords will be on a draw breath.

On BETTER DAY dig the slight warble effect during the first instrumental chorus (on the return from the tonic to the subdominant)...and notice that the run which works through the dominant pattern is a variation of the one you learned from BAD LUCK BLUES. You can hear that all of Sonny's runs fit into the tonal patterns of the guitar chords, even though each individual note may not be part of the chord itself.

Dig the hand tremolo on the tonic part of the instrumental chorus of DARK ROAD.

The phrase (in the harp chorus after the "steel driving" chords) on JOHN HENRY goes something like this:

dah	du	dooo	dooo
4 ▼	5 ▲	6 ▲	6 ▲

da-dooo	da-doo	doo	da-doo
5▲ 6▲	5▲ 6▲	6▲	5▼ 4▼

da-doo	doo	da-doo	da-doo
5▲ 6▲	6▲	5▲ 6▲	5▲ 6▲

("ma--ma's knee")

doo	doo	ooo	waaah
6▲	5▼	5▲	4▼

This is not a literal transcription (some of the single notes are actually half-chords)--but its close enough to play out okay, and give you an idea of what is going on. Right now is a good time for you to figure these things out for your own self--you'll learn more and faster, and then you can sneer at the book which oughta be good for your ego. See if you can figure out the high note "explosion" in the second instrumental chorus.

On MAKE A LITTLE MONEY notice the hand tremolo effect again, this time on the dominant run at the end of the first instrumental chorus. Keep your ears open for this tremolo on other cuts--he uses it every now and then.

Try to figure out the rhythm pattern on OLD JABO--remember that it's built on the basic "dit dit dah dah" in and out pattern...except that a lot of little decoration is added. If you can't get it all at full speed, slow it down to 16 and try again. If it doesn't come after a fair amount of work, go on to something else and come back later.

Notice how on GUITAR HIGHWAY Sonny plays around with the melody--sometimes he's with it, then he leaves for a run that weaves around it, and then returns again--usually with chords.

Hear that weird guitar chord in HEART IN SORROW?? See if you can follow the changes.

Try working out the rhythm to BOOGIE BABY -- it's one Sonny uses frequently. But don't try to get all of this in one sitting. Take your time man--remember it took Sonny years to get to where he is--don't expect to be able to do it in a week or two.

Summing up: Sonny's main characteristics are complex rhythms, single note melodic runs (often in counterpoint), falsetto-vocal harp interweaving, and heavy rhythm chords, cut-off sharply.

Of course there's a hell of a lot more to it than this--but it's up to you to find it. I could maybe tell you, but you're much better off discovering and understanding it for yourself--that way it belongs to you. From here on, you're on your own--just remember that most effects are built on a basic foundation--know the foundation, and with practice you should be able to get most anybody's style. But don't stop at just duplicating somebody else's style--make your own!

Sonny Boy Williamson I

Sonny Boy Williamson I
and Big Bill Broonzy

Photo by George Addius/Courtesy
of Blues Classics Records

In the work of Sonny Boy I you can hear the gap between country or "folk" and city styles being bridged. Sonny Boy was a very influential cat, and most of the harp men to appear on the scene after him owe him a big debt.

Unfortunately, most of his best work isn't readily available. These sides with Big Joe William on Bluebird and Columbia were originally on 78's and as of this writing no plans have been made to reissue them in LP form. On these sides he was working solely as a sideman and since he had more time to develop his ideas (not needing to sing) the harp is often fantastic.

However, an LP with a cross section of his work from 1937-44 has been issued--SONNY BOY WILLIAMSON (Blues Classics, Box 5073, Berkeley 5, Calif.) the backing ranges from guitar and mandolin to his full band with piano, bass, guitar and drums.

First, just sit down and dig it once without using your harp. Notice here too that most of the effects and techniques used are ones you already know--it's the manner in which he uses them which makes up his style. You'll note that Sonny Boy works mostly in a straight 12-bar tonic-subdominant-dominant form, with fairly simple rhythms, and that the beat is heavily emphasized. The harp stays with the beat, rather than playing counterpoint to it as Sonny Terry often does. Sonny Boy's major characteristics are the "crying" choked chords and the "wah-wah" vocal sounds. He plays mostly single note runs on the instrumental breaks--and these runs are more often based on the chord progressions than the melody of the song--except on the older guitar-backed numbers, where the harp had to carry more of the melody line. First, try this pattern--Sonny Boy uses it (or variations built from it) in almost every number he recorded:

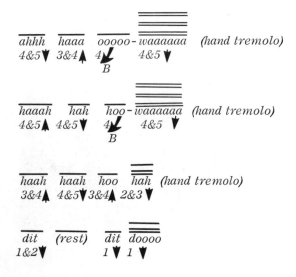

Rather than being four separate phrases, this should be played as almost a continuous phrase in itself. The accent (or beat) comes on the first chord of each phrase. The tremolos begin as soon as you hit the notes marked--in the first phrase for example, the tremolo should start as soon as you open up to the draw chord on holes #4 and #5. Try tapping your foot every three time units--in the first phrase tap once on the "ahhh", twice on the "waaaaaa" (the six lines above means six time units, remember?--or, this note lasts six times as long as the preceeding ones)...and so on for the other phrases. Part of Sonny Boy's style is this heavy emphasis on a straightforward, relatively uncomplicated beat. Where "hand tremolo" is marked you should be using the "throat" or "glottal stop" tremolo method as well, at the same time. On the "ooooo/waaaaaaa" part of the phrase it should sound as if the single note (#4 hole, draw and bend) is mushrooming up and open to the chord (#4 and #5 draw)--with the tremolo beginning as soon as the chord starts to sound--this is how the "crying" sound is made. Try this phrase a few times. If you can't get it here, dig the opening cut on the record--Sonny Boy uses this phrase (or something close to it) as a run through the dominant introductory phrases.

According to my machine (which don't lie a lot) here are the harp keys used:

SIDE ONE				SIDE TWO			
1) D		5) C		1) D		5) C	
2) C		6) C		2) C		6) B-flat	
3) D		7) B-flat		3) B-flat		7) C--first position	
4) D		8) B-flat		4) C		8) B-flat	

All of these harps are played in cross position except for the one marked first. (Here's how you can tell it's first: the backing is in C, right? So try a cross with it using an F harp. It sounds a little high-pitched, though it seems to work--but the real tip-off is in the "dit dit duuu" phrase he uses as a kickoff point for the next verse. Usually the last note of that little phrase is the strongest. In second position it's a draw note in the first hole--but it sounds weaker here--indicating that he isn't in second position. So try first and you find that the melody runs played between lines of the lyric can be played in this position. Also, dig the final chord--it sounds more like a first position than a crossed chord. And the final consideration is that this cut was recorded in 1941--and in those days F harps were probably a lot scarcer than they are now. So it's first position. This same method works for other artists as well--remember that the position used was usually determined by two main things; whichever worked best to get the various effects needed--and which key harps the man had with him at the time of the recording.)

By the way, here's the run between the lyric lines of SLOPPY DRUNK:

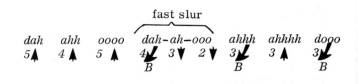

This is about a bitch to play--going from #5 to #4 draw-and-bend and right to #3 draw ain't easy--and that slur has to be awfully fast. Work with it--see if you can cut it. If you flat can't, try this: it's a cop-out--but it approximates the run:

In this substitute phrase, one of the notes from the triplet is dropped (you can hardly hear the damn thing anyway) and the draw and bend note follows right after the two-note slur. Whichever way you do it, dig that the last note of the phrase "dooooo" returns part way to a straight #3 hole draw note. What I mean: he begins to bend it back up to its normal pitch, then cuts it off while it's still bent--either right after the bend begins, or when it's halfway back to its normal pitch. Ain't that a groovy little run???

Go through the LP and try playing along. Notice that Sonny Boy doesn't chop off his chords as Sonny Terry does--instead they just sort of die away. Dig the frequent use of the "dit dit/duuu" phrase, and "choked" chords that open out, with the tremolo "crying" sound.

COLLECTOR MAN is one of Sonny Boy's earliest recordings, and is in more of a country vein than his later work--the harp plays more melody here and is a bit more mournful. UNTIL MY LOVE COMES DOWN is in the same vein, as is YOU GIVE AN ACCOUNT which has something of a jug-band flavor to it--notice the raw, raucous chords in the instrumental chorus. Dig the "wah-wah" chords in WESTERN UNION MAN. They are done by using the elbow as the pivot, and swinging the whole hand towards and away from the cup. Notice how this intensifies the sound, and gives a more urgent effect. Try duplicating the break on SHOTGUN BLUES--the "wah-wah" sound here uses both the hands and words formed with the mouth and tongue. (By the way the reason this number sounds familiar is that Big Joe Williams recorded it several times under titles like SHE LEFT ME A MULE TO RIDE.) Dig the beautiful harp on BAD LUCK BLUES...notice that here he's cutting off the chords a bit more sharper than on other numbers. Sonny Boy has a unique vocal phrasing which is often imitated--but much of it is due to the fact that he had a bad stutter (you can hear it a bit on JIVING THE BLUES.) Try to duplicate the rhythm and melody breaks on this cut. (I could diagram it out, but you'll learn 69 times as much figuring it out for yourself.) In SLOPPY DRUNK BLUES the "dit dit/duuu" phrase is played with the first "dit" dropped. (In first position it's #3 hole blow, coming from the tonic note of #4 hole blow--straight??)

Summing up: Sonny Boy's main characteristics are "choked" notes that open into "crying" chords, simple rhythm and simple melody runs, and various "wah-wah" effects. Of course, this only scrapes the surface of his style, but by working with the record you should be able to figure out the basics of it.

Lemme say it again (try and stop me)-- understand his style, then go on and use what you need to make your own thing. (As I write this there's a lonesome train whistle out the window--A harp, crossed by the way--god, but that's a sad sound on a rainy night...) In other words, absorb, ingest, osmosize, steal, borrow, gulp, grip and gargle what you need from various styles to help you say your own thing. I think that's what's called the folk-process of assimilation...or some such shit.

Sonny Boy Williamson II (Rice Miller)

Sonny Boy Williamson II   Photo by Bob Koester
Courtesy of Delmark Records

As far as I'm concerned, this Sonny Boy was the all-time, non-stop BOSS of bluesharp--so it's a little hard to write objectively about his style. And it's not only his harp--it's his songs and the way he sings them--for my bread, he was one of the top bluesmen, period.

At this writing, Sonny Boy's best sides aren't available on LP. (I just got word that Blues Classics will issue an LP of 16 early sides recorded in Mississippi in 1951-54--including the fantastic Mighty Long Time--probably in late 1965. DON'T MISS THIS!) But until then, we'll have to use the only LP on the market, DOWN AND OUT BLUES (Checker 1437). It's made up of singles released on the Chicago label from sessions recorded in 1955-57.

Once again, the first thing to do is just sit down and dig it. You'll notice that the backing is straight R&B, but that his harp is more "down-home". It has the same intensity that Mississippi guitar bluesmen use in the delta style of blues--yet it blends in perfectly with the more modern R&B sound, to make a hell of an effective style of music.

Notice that Rice uses some of the same

techniques as the original Sonny Boy; fairly straight-forward rhythms, short single note phrases for runs, and the "crying" sound. He has given a lot more emphasis to the "wah-wah" effect and uses it more often--and the same goes for hand tremolo effects on chords. Another main characteristic is his intensity--his harp was the most mournful, vocal-sounding around... he played for keeps. (But don't make the mistake of confusing volume with intensity--harp can be very slow and quiet, yet still insistent as hell.) The instrumental choruses with the harp seem to be based about equally on melody and the chord progressions of a number--he improvises on the mood of the piece.

Rice also leaves "holes" in the harp runs for the backing to come through--and this is another important thing. Good harpmen know that there are times when the best sound you can make is none-- usually beginners tend to fill in every space with chords or intricate runs--but often a pause, so that you can appreciate the harp all the more when it returns, is twice as effective. Once again--it's the feel of a piece that counts--not how many notes were were played. Another thing both Sonny Boys have in common is the "dit dit duuu" phrase used as punctuation between verses or lines of verses.

Here's how the tunings check out on my machine:

SIDE ONE

    1) C   4) F

    2) C Third position   5) C

    3) C   6) E fourth position (or chromatic in C#)

SIDE TWO

    1) E   4) B-flat

    2) B-flat   5) F

    3) G   6) C

The above are harp keys--all are in second position, unless otherwise marked. The last cut on side one could be either one of the two named--both work--but I suspect that he's using a chromatic--the notes are easier to find on a chromatic. (Sounds like a Hohner Chromonica tuned in C.)

Now go through one time, and try playing along with the record. Try to get with his phrasing. Notice that he cuts off the "wah-wahs" with his tongue about the same way we've been cutting off chords-- they don't sound as chopped off because they're single notes. Try playing along with I DON'T KNOW in third position. The opening "wah-wah" is on holes #5 and #4, draw--alternating from #5 to #4. The harp chorus begins the same way--here's the whole thing:

(Tonic)

Aaaaaaa--waaaaaah   (hand tremolo)
5 ▼   4▼

Aaaaaaa (tremolo)   dow dow dow dow (all cut
5▼   4▼ 4▼ 4▼ 4▼ sharply)

(Subdominant)

Ahhh waa waaa waaa Ahh hah ah hah
5▼   4▼ 4▼   4▼   5▼ 5▲ 4▼ 3▲

waaah   waaaa (tremolo)
2↙   1▼
B

(Dominant)

waaaah (tremolo) ahooooo   ooooo   ah-waaaaaaah
3↙   5 ▼   5 ▲   3▼ 4▼
B

Those four sharp "dow dow dow dow" notes in the tonic phrase all have a slight bend on them--they are cut off almost as soon as the bend begins. If you can't hear how the tremolo's work in, slow down your phono to "16" one time.

Try to get Sonny Boy's "wah-wah" sound. Actually, it comes closer to being "ab-waah" much of the time. Work on bending a single note, then cutting it off with your tongue while it's still bent. Notice that the "dit dit/duuu" phrase of Sonny Boy- comes out in Rice's style as something like "ab-waah waa-waa waa-waa waaah dit/duuu"--and it's usually done on #3 hole blow (except for the "dit/duuu" notes, which are holes 1 and 2 draw.)

Try ALL MY LOVE IN VAIN one time. Shape the "ab-waa's" with your mouth and use your hand to close the cup at the end of the cut-off bent notes. The groovy bends in the harp chorus are on either the 2nd or 3rd holes in--this is one of Sonny Boy's favorite sounds. Work on this whole song, trying to get as close to the actual notes as you can--Sonny Boy is close to his best here, and most of his style shows up in this one number--the bends, tremolos, phrasing technique and "talking" sounds can all be clearly heard here.

The KEY shows how effective notes held a long time can be--when used in the right place. Dig the warble-bend on the second tonic phrase of the harp chorus--it's a chord on holes #4 and #5 draw; first straight draw, then bent, then straight again, with a slight warble all the way through. And did you catch that long bent note that slides up on the transition from the tonic to the subdominant? (#2 hole in again.) By the way, the last note of the song is over-dubbed... he doesn't really have two mouths.

On DISSATISFIED, Sonny Boy is playing amplified harp (holding a PA mike in his hands, with the harp cupped on top--plugged in to his own amplifier) which accounts for the different tone of the harp heard here. I'm not positive, but I'm pretty sure he's using a chromatic harp in C tuning. Since the backing is in G# he has to be playing in either G# or C#--and the easiest way to get these keys is on a chromatic with the slide pressed in. (See the chromatic harp section.) However, you can come pretty close by using an E harp in fourth position...try it one time for the practice. (Suspect it's a chromatic because it doesn't have Sonny Boy's usual sound; there are fewer bent notes, fewer "ab-waaa's"--and the main reason could be that it's a chromatic harp-- which has reeds that are harder to work with.) If you've got both kinds of harps--pick your favorite.

On FATTENING FROGS FOR SNAKES the "ab-waaa's" are usually on the 2nd hole draw (on the phrases used as punctuation)--often when Sonny Boy is using a higher-pitched harp (E or F) he'll do it this way, since the out notes being higher pitched are a little shriller.

WAKE UP BABY has more of a call-and-response pattern to it than appears in most on Sonny Boy's work. Dig the heavy use of hand tremolo on YOUR FUNERAL AND MY TRIAL. On both CROSS MY HEART and "99" Sonny Boy is using amplified harp again--notice that it gets in his way some--he works better with both hands free.

Try working out with this LP. Learn his phrasing and timing--it's boss! And try to get hold of some of the more recent Checker singles. They're almost all good but LONESOME CABIN (Checker 956), TRUST MY BABY (963), and HELP ME (1036) are outstanding. On some of these sides (963 is one) Sonny Boy uses the big Marine Band--#365 in G tuning...and the way he plays it it sounds almost like a cello sometimes. This harp has longer and heavier reeds than the smaller models and it's good for lead work.

To sum up: Sonny Boy II uses frequent "ab-waaa" effects, with cut-off bent notes, short phrases and single note runs, and tremolos and both chords and single notes. And he plays like he means every note. Maybe that's why he was so great--he did.

Little Walter

Little Walter set the style for R&B harp and he is much imitated. At first he played much like the first Sonny Boy Williamson, but as he worked with Muddy Waters he began to evolve his own, distinctive

Little Walter - Best known of the Chicago harpmen.

style. (You can hear it happening on THE BEST OF MUDDY WATERS--Chess LP 1427). His earlier work, play unamplified was a good deal "busier"-- he played more rhythm and runs, leaving few holes unfilled. But when he started to use amplified harp regularly, his style began to change--becoming more fluid and almost jazz-like. But it wasn't until he left Muddy and formed his own group and played instrumentals that he reached the peak of his ability.

For reference let's use THE BEST OF LITTLE WALTER (Chess LP 1428) which contains some of his best early vocals and four instrumentals. First thing to do, of course, is just sit down and dig it. You'll notice that his style has the usual amount of basic blues harp technique, but he has added his own effects. He uses tremolo and warble a lot, and many multi-noted short runs which are often based more on the changes than on the actual melody of the number. (His counterpart is B. B. King who was the most influential of the R&B guitarists.) On some numbers he uses his "big axe"-the 64 Chromonica. His style is shaped somewhat by the fact that he can't use his hands to mold sounds (as he's holding the harp and mike in both)--so a good deal of the forming of sound is done in the mouth.

I'll be straight--I've never met Little Walter or seen him work--so all of the following is based entirely on his recordings, and talks with people who do know him. I can't be absolutely positive which numbers are played with a chromatic harp and which aren't--but I've made some guesses which should be close. (One reason that it's hard to tell is that amplified harp sounds a good deal different from unamplified--by fooling with tone controls and such you can get some pretty hairy sounds out of even the little Marine Bands. In most cases, the numbers in question can be played either on a chromatic or Marine Band--the difference is in the ease of playing and-slightly-in the chords obtained.) In any event, here are the tunings:

SIDE ONE

1) B-flat   4) G

2) B-flat (chromatic) 5) D

3) A   6) C

SIDE TWO

1) A   4) B-flat (chromatic
                                       (???) in F)

2) B-flat (chromatic
   (??) in F)   5) G ?????

3) C   6) C

The above are harp keys, all in second position--except where the chromatic is used. Now go through the LP one time and try playing along... try to get inside his phrasing. It'd be best to hold the harp with both hands, one on either side, to approximate the way he holds it with a mike. Dig the hard warbles with the hand on the subdominant phrase of MY BABE--he uses a warble effect on almost every chord, but they're especially noticable here. (By the way, a lot of Chicago harpmen, rather than move the harp and heavy PA mike back and forth just hold it steady and shake their heads for the warbles--but it just gives me a headache.)

The deeper, echo-y sound on SAD HOURS is what leads me to believe that it's a chromatic. This can also be played on a B-flat Marine Band-- try both and pick your favorite. Notice how the hard, "meaner" notes later on contrast with the fluid, melancholy sound of the opening chords. Little Walter has a great sense of "dynamics"--by dynamics here I mean the differences of effect that various methods of playing notes gives. He uses a variety of "attacks" to get the results he wants-- making notes "hard" or "soft", runs fluid or stacatto. For lead harp work this is something you'll have to know--use the contrasts in sound to help the mood.

LAST NIGHT is another piece where the harp carries the mood of the song beautifully... dig how single notes alternate with tremolo chords.

Dig the call-and-response opening to BLUES WITH A FEELING...and notice how the tremolo is carried through both parts of the tonic of the harp chorus--while the subdominant and dominant progressions are played as runs.

CAN'T HOLD OUT MUCH LONGER was one of Little Walter's earlier solo recordings--and the stacatto style that he used to use still shows through somewhat--the tone is a bit more raucous than on his later sides. And the same is true of JUKE. Listen to how he opens it in the second octave (using #6 hole blow a lot) and then runs down to the usual cross position in the first octave. And dig that long passage all on #4 hole draw...and the way he works in little rhythm chords--almost as an after-thought. Play through this number until you can duplicate it pretty closely--it contains most of the elements of his basic style.

MEAN OLD WORLD is a toss-up between Marine Band and chromatic--it works either way. (It's easier for me on a Marine Band, but thats probably because I've played a hell of a lot more on them than on chromatics.) Take your pick. Notice that there's a lot of tremolo or warble here again.

Dig the single note work in the front of OFF THE WALL--it's in holes #2 and #3. Here again rhythm chords are used, but they stay in the background, rather than coming on strong in front. Dig the dynamics at work here.

YOU'D BETTER WATCH YOURSELF could also be a chromatic. Whichever it is, there's some groovy phrasing on the instrumental chorus.

The accompaniment for BLUE LIGHTS is in D, so I'd normally figure a G harp is being used in second position...but I've been told by a cat who knows Walter that he used a harp with special tuning (possibly the Marine Band soloist--which is arranged in a chromatic style of tuning without a slide.) My-self, I always thought it was the 64 Chromatic--what do you think??? Whatever the hell it is--it's a boss cut!!

TELL ME MAMA could be chromatic-- almost every number could, for that matter. Why not try 'em all on a chromatic?? Remember you have to use your tongue to bend notes on the chromatic... and, if you're using that big 64 mother you'll probably want to make the warble sound by moving your head back and forth, instead of moving the harp.

To sum-up: Little Walter uses a lot of hard tremolo/warble chords, alternating with almost jazz-like runs...and the dynamics of playing are very important to the overall sound. Some of the tonal effects are due to attachments on the amplifiers such as revereberation (echo) units, and the majority of the effects are produced by the mouth and lips, since the hands are busy holding the harp and mike.

Again, there's a hell of a lot more to it than this little taste--you could write a book this size about R&B harp styles alone--and I hope some-body will someday. In the meantime, listen. Check out some Muddy Waters singles--he has had some of the finest R&B harpmen around recording with him at one time or another--such people as Junior Wells,

Little Walter, Shakey Walter Horton, and James Cotton can all be heard. Of course, once you've done a lot of listening and got the sounds inside your head, the best way to get straight is to play them out. Sit in anywhere you can--even R&R bands use changes that'll work with Chicago-styled harp. And you can't really get Chicago harp sounds by playing accoustically--you should be playing with an amplifier. And if you get the chance, dig the people in person--one night in a South Side bar is worth two weeks with records.

Jimmy Reed

Jimmy Reed   Photo by Raeburn Flerlage

Jimmy Reed is a full circle within himself. He blends both deep country and Chicago R&B influences to make his own, unique sound--a sound of right now. His overall sound is that of lazy, relaxed yet insistent blues. Much of the time he understates--his harp is unamplified and sparse--but effective as hell.

Ever since he began his recording career in 1953 he has played both harp and guitar together. His band lineup usually consists of rhythm guitar, bass guitar and drums--Jimmy plays lead guitar and harp (in a rack, around his neck) himself. He has a lot of LP's available on the Vee-Jay label--let's use the one called JIMMY REED: THE LEGEND--THE MAN (VJ 8501). It's based on a hit-a-year idea, and the twelve cuts include his bigest selling songs from 1953-64.

First, dig it. Notice that he works with a very basic rhythm pattern--and almost all of his numbers are variations of the same bass line. You can hear the progressions and changes very easily-- and for this reason Reed is probably one of the best recording bluesmen to learn from. The fact that his harp is in a rack and his hands are busy with the guitar has something to do with shaping his harp style--but choice has as much to do with it as necessity. He plays harp mostly single-note style with very few chords--and his phrasing is very laconic. The harp choruses are usually close to the melody, or in counterpoint to it--and he usually plays with or on the rhythm, as opposed to around it or against it. In his more recent recordings he tends to use higher notes--one reason is that unamplified harp gets hard to hear on gigs where everything else is going full-blast and higher-pitched notes carry better-but again, choice comes into it too. Dig that sometimes the harp comes in between lines of verse in a modified call-and-response shot, while other times it just punctuates.

Here are the tunings, based on an average between two machines (it's not quite right on either):

SIDE ONE

1)	A	4)	A
2)	B-flat	5)	A-first Position
3)	B-flat	6)	A-first Position

SIDE TWO

1)	A	4)	no harp--backing in G
2)	A	5)	A
3)	A first position	6)	A-first Position

Let's go through it now one time. If you don't have a rack (most music stores sell one that fits around your neck called Elton Harmonica Holder #5520 for about $1.25), play with both hands holding the harp--or sit on one of them--no hand effects are used.

HIGH AND LONESOME was Reed's first recording for Vee-Jay, and he plays more harp on this number than on more recent ones...it comes in requently between lines of verses. Dig that he plays mostly "straightforward" notes--he doesn't bend often, and uses almost none of the "wah-wah" or other vocal effects most harpmen use. Also, he tends to drop the harp on the transitional dominant run back to the tonic--probably so that he'll be ready to sing the next verse. Try playing along. Get your notes clean and easy.

YOU DON'T HAVE TO GO is a fine example of understated harp--the pauses and holes he leaves are as much a part of his style as the notes he does play--it all contributes to the overall sound he wants. The tremolo on the subdominant phrase of the harp chorus sounds as though he's shaking his head slightly from side to side to make it. Try to get his exact phrasing here. Like the man says, it helps if you don't drink hard liquor.

AIN'T THAT LOVING YOU BABY is one of Reed's drivingest numbers--and one of the first R&B sides with harp that turned me on in front. Here he plays around with the standard form a bit: he switches back and forth from the tonic to dominant during the verses, while the subdominant sneaks in on the choruses...and during the instrumental harp breaks it goes into the usual tonic-subdominant-dominant form--switching back again for the vocal. Dig Reed's "attack" on the harp here-he hits those notes <u>hard</u> Mel, --in fact he sometimes ruins a harp a number by flatting out the reeds from blowing too hard. It's best if you take it a little cooler though-- unless you happen to have a crate of harps sitting around. Dig how clean his notes are--sharp and distinct single tones.

On both HONEST I DO and GOING TO NEW YORK Jimmy plays an A harp in first position (it seems whenever the backing is in A he'll use an A harp rather than cross a D)--which accounts for the high notes--usually in the #7-#10th holes.

HONEST I DO plays with thé structure again. Dig the first verse (after the instrumental intro): it begins on the tonic, goes to the dominant, returns to the tonic briefly, goes through the subdominant, back to the dominant and returns to the tonic agaon. After this one-time-only pattern, the subdominant is dropped altogether and the form is tonic-dominant-tonic. (This is the form used behind all harp choruses.) Here's an almost literal transcription of the harp chorus following the first verse:

doo !	*doo!*	*doo*	*a*	*woo*	*ooooo*
8↑	8↑	8↑	8↑ (B)	8↑	7↑

doo	*doo*	*ooo*	*ah*	*doo*	*ooo*
8↑	8↑	9↓	8↑	8↑ (B)	8↓

doo	*waa*	*doo-ooooooo*		*ah*
9↑ (B)	9↑	9↑ (B)	9↑	9↑ (B)

doo	*ooo*	*doo-oooo*	*ooo-doo-ah*			*dooo*
9↓	9↑	8↑	8↑ (B)	7↑	8↓	7↑	6&7↑

Try this -- you'll see that you have to use a lot of wind and hit the notes hard and carefully to control the "out" bends. If you can't make bent notes on the #9 hole blow in the third phrase above, substitute #8 draw for bent #9's--it's not quite the same, but sounds pretty close. Both of the "doo" notes at the front of the first phrase are hit hard and bent slightly...and the triplet fast-slur in the last phrase makes the last four notes sound like three. Try following the vocal melody line in your head while playing this break—you'll see the harp sticks fairly close to it.

GOING TO NEW YORK is in a standard progression, and the harp is up in the same range again. Dig that in first position in that octave the tonic note is #7 hole blow--subdominant is #9 draw-- and dominant is #9 hole blow--but you'll notice that Jimmy doesn't always stick to this basic setup. Here he uses the dominant note through the tonic phrases-- but it works--when you get up to reeds pitched that high you can screw around more.

Sometimes when he's in the key of A Jimmy will stay in the higher octaves through the tonic and subdominant phrases, and then drop down to the #2, #3 and #4 holes for the tonic-subdominant resolving phrases--it's a nice contrast. (Dig BABY WHATS ON YOUR MIND on Vee-Jay LP 1008-- ROCKING WITH REED.)

(On a few numbers that Reed has recorded elsewhere, the backing is in B--and usually Jimmy plays an A harp in third position for them...but more often he plays crossed or first position.)

Dig that on the first two numbers of the second side (and usually when the backing is in E or F) Jimmy sticks to the lower octaves. Try following along. BRIGHT LIGHTS is in first position again, and he's up in the last octave once more. AW SHUCKS HUSH YOUR MOUTH doesn't have any harp on it--so it's a good chance for you to really work out--pick any style or position you want to try...you got a good solid background to work with here.

To sum up: Reed's harp is laconic in phrasing, but hard in attack. He leaves many holes for the backing to fill in, and uses pauses for emphasis. His harp breaks are usually close to the melody or in a counterpoint to it. When the backing is in A he almost always plays first position.

Dig his other LP's--and the singles that haven't been reissued as yet. And the same thing as before, one time more--you got to listen and play both. It won't fall into your lap man--you got to shake the tree some!

13

Solo or Lead Harp Vs. Accompanying

In the last year or two I've heard a lot of good, young kids playing blues harp--but most of them make one big mistake--they try to lead when they're accompanying a singer. You can't do both-- it's one or the other.

If you play solo, groovy--you're on your own and you can ring changes every bar if you want and play 17-bar runs if you like. Solo harp, without any backing is free as hell--limited only by musical form (if you want to play blues you're limited some- what to the basic blues form) and your imagination.

If you plan to lead a group that's another thing--in group work you have to stick fairly close to a standard form--or you have instead of a group a bunch of soloists fighting each other. Remember that music is a total thing--and the whole sound counts--not just the sound you make.

Now, about accompanying. If you're back- ing a guitarist you should be doing just that--backing. It shouldn't be a fight between you and him to see who comes out on top. If it is, maybe you should lead your own group or play solo--music shouldn't be a competition. And I have heard so many good songs ruined because every sideman was trying to be the whole damn show--that ain't the way it works, baby. A song has a mood or a story to tell. Your job as a harpman is to help tell that story or transmit that mood. You have to feel it first and communicate it second. Sure it's a temptation to use some flashy technique and come on strong--but if it draws at- tention more to the technique than to what the music is trying to say it's no goddam good--you'd be better off to just stand and shout "HEY EVERYBODY DIG ME--I'M GROOVY!" Remember technique is only a means, not an end. And if you let technique get to be an end in itself you're missing the whole point of music. I'm not saying you should ignore it--you need it to communicate--but you should be able to communicate more than what an accomplished technician you are...otherwise, whats the difference between you and an IBM machine hooked up to a harp with an air hose??

There are two main ways to accompany--by form and by instinct. If you're playing with people who stick to a standard 12-bar form than you can work either off the changes or the melody--chording during the vocal, making runs between lines and doing what you want on the instrumental breaks...or whatever style you use. Just so that you remember that the words are important--and harp that is too loud or too flashy during the verses soon gets to be a pain in the ass to hear. Work out an accompaniment that fits the mood of a song--a slow, mournful blues shouldn't have bouncy bright little runs hopping around inside it--and a jump number shouldn't be full of long crying tones. (That's a generalization--there are exceptions to every rule. But it's mostly valid.) Remember--you're trying to tell somebody something-- and if all you tell is how well you can play the harp then why dontcha join the Harmonicats???

Playing by instinct is necessary when you play with people who extend the form, change and bend it around...taking sometimes 12-bar verses, sometimes 16-bar. The only way to really accompany somebody like that is to know their head--to <u>feel</u>

what's going to happen, before it does. In other words, you have to <u>know</u> when the changes will come-- not by time measures, but by the mood--and you got to be ready for them with notes that fit. Playing with people like this becomes a matter of improvising on mood and feel more than on changes, and the only way it works is for you to know how your partner sees the sounds.

A few general thoughts:

When playing with somebody you've never heard before, try chording along on just the progression until you dig his style--then you can step out more.

Leave holes for the guitar to fill--don't try to cram notes into every pause in a vocal.

<u>Listen</u> to what your partner is playing and try to build from that--and he should do the same for you--it should be an interchange scene--if you're partners and not rivals.

Know when to shut up entirely. Some numbers just don't need harp on them and playing with them only screws up the sound.

Make your style appropriate to the music being played. (I heard a kid trying to play Sonny Terry harp with Son House who was singing a straight delta blues--didn't make it at all!)

In short be a sideman or a leader--but only one at a time.

14

Harp Care

Yes, babies, it's best to take care of your harps--maybe in your old age they'll do something nice for you. A few tips follow.

Breaking In

All new harps need breaking in before you can really wail with them. New reeds are stiff and hard to work with. Besides, if you take the time to break 'em in right, you'll get more use out of them.

When you first get a new harp, start out by playing it very gently--don't bend notes at all at first. Just play chords and runs for a while, using very little breath to begin with, then gradually increase it. (Blow hard on a new harp and you can permanently 'flat out' reeds). After you've loosened up the reeds by simple playing, make some easy bends--once again, using only a little wind--just as much as is necessary to make the bends work. As the reeds loosen up further you can gradually increase your wind until you're playing as you normally would. Rather than trying to do this in one sitting, it's best to spread it out a little over a few days-- playing say ten or fifteen minutes a day. Sure it takes time to do this, but it's worth it because you'll get more out of a harp. The bends will be smoother and hold the true pitch longer.

Once you get used to playing you'll be able to find your own harps easily, by the way they're broken in--everybody breaks in harps to his own style; certain notes that are more frequently used will play easier, certain bends will work better, etc. For this reason it's a good idea to keep new harps to yourself until they're broken in to your style. You can tell that a new harp is ready to go when you can bend notes without collapsing your lungs, and when the reeds feel as though they're all yours--instead of being part of an external thing. You'll know when it happens.

And of course the usual jazz about keeping it clean goes here too--playing with a mouthful of peanuts or glue is a drag. And it won't hurt to wipe off the mouthpiece when you're finished playing, either--otherwise a layer of dead skin and crud builds up. Doesn't really hurt anything, but it's nauseating. The main thing to remember about breathing in is to be cool at first--don't blow your mind and reeds at the same time.

Soaking Harps

To soak or not to soak--that is the question? I've heard arguments both ways--on the minus side: it makes them rusty, the wood swells, making it harder on your lips, and it shortens harp life some.

On the plus side soaking gives greater volume with less wind, loosens the reeds and makes bends easier--and generally makes it easier to play.

So it's up to you to decide which is more important--long life or playing ease. Myself, I (and almost every other harpman I know who plays un-amplified harp) prefer to soak them. A whole night full of hard driving, full volume wailing is almost impossible without soaking--most cats just don't have the wind to make it. And soaking helps to carry the harp sound over a 12-string or other loud instruments.

There are several ways to go about it. Some prefer to wet the harp just once (under a faucet) when they're breaking it in. Run the water in the mouthpiece side until it's good and saturated, then slap it out on your hand to unclog the reeds. Usually a couple of good slaps with the back (sound side) down, followed by a couple of crossways taps (with the top of the harp parallel to your hand) will do it. Then blow all the way through it to make sure the reeds are clear of water. You can tell it's wet enough when it "sings" when you slap it across your hand.

I usually keep a glass of water around when I'm playing and soak each harp just before I

use it. (A glass of vodka is nice if you got the bread.) If a harp gets too wet I find that the tone changes slightly--it goes sharp some--and with a 12-string that can be a major disaster--so I just soak them as I need them.

Others keep all their harps constantly in water, tapping them out as needed and replacing when done.

Like I say, it depends on your needs. For one or two easy numbers, soaking isn't really necessary--but when you got to play long and loud it helps like hell. (At parties, in an emergency, you can soak harps with a mouthful of beer--but this makes 'em sticky, and usually dribbles on the floor. Depends on how much beer there is, how fast you need to soak, and how up tight the owner is about his floor.)

Soaking does shorten the life of a harp somewhat, so balance it on your own scale. And there's one other hassle--continual wetting of the wood causes it to swell and bow out, so that it sticks out as much as an eighth of an inch beyond the mouthpiece. If you've got sensitive lips, it's best to shave the wood so that it's even with the metal again. You can either cut off the protruding edges with a very sharp knife (like an Exacto), or if you're the patient type, use sandpaper--but unless you want a lungful of sawdust, hold the harp mouthpiece side down while you're sanding. Myself, I find all that more hassle than it's worth--so it's up to you.

Prolonging Life

Of harps that is. In time, all harps, no matter how well broken-in and cared for, are gonna wear out. (To give you an idea, of the keys used regularly, I wear out a Marine Band every month and a half--that's playing two or three nights a week, three hours or more a night.)

When a harp goes bad, one of two main things happens.

The first is; it loses its true pitch. Certain notes that are frequently bent (#2 hole draw for example) will eventually get used to being bent--and when you play them normally will still sound a little flat. So some reeds will be in the correct pitch, others will be out. When this happens, the easiest thing to do is just junk the harp.

Some musical instrument repairers will fix them,--but the honest ones will tell you in front that it'll cost more than the harp is worth--unless you got a big chromatic. I know some people who file their own reeds, but since you got to be damn near a Stradivarius to do that, the best solution when certain reeds go out of pitch is to get a new harp.

The other main thing that happens is that reeds 'flat out'--that is, they get stuck so you can't get any sound out of them. Again, the easiest thing to do is just replace the harp—but if you're going to toss it anyway, try this first: Get a pan of water and heat till it's almost boiling, then put the harp in with tongs (unless you're a masochist, in which case use your hands) for a minute or two. Then take it out and immediately run cold water over and through it. What happens is that heat expands the frame inside, and the reeds as well--but (since they are of different materials and weight) not at the same rate. So when the cold water contracts these metals, sometimes the reeds will contract faster than the casing-- and in doing so, will free themselves. If it doesn't work the first time, try it again. Sometimes two or three boilings are necessary. (By the way, make sure you use a pot that's easy to clean--the paint on the back of the harp usually comes off all over the place. Also, you'll see little globs of junk floating around in the water...that's all the stuff that has been trapped in the reeds. But don't get up tight-- even clean-mouthed people have dirty harps.)

Or try this: take the metal outer cover of the harp off. You only need to take off the cover over the offending reed. Remember that the top (or numbered) side covers the blow reeds and the bottom (trademark) side covers the draw reeds. The plates are held on by nails which look like screws--but don't mess with a screwdriver 'cause you won't get anywhere. Just pry the covers off as carefully as possible, trying not to bend the nails. When the cover is off, dig your loused up reed. Usually what has happened is that it catches on one side or the other of the channel that is cut in the case for it to vibrate in. Sometimes you can just twist it slightly (from the end it's attached at) to free it, other times filing

may be necessary. But when you file (either along an edge or at the free end) remember that you're taking away some of its weight--and weight as well as length determines the pitch of a reed. So if you file much at all, you'll change the tone--which'll screw the whole works up. Try bending the reed back to its proper angle to the metal plate that it's mounted on. Sometimes it will get bent too much, and too much or too little angle will make it hard to play. The best way is to try different angles and see which works best. Once you got it working right, put the cover back on. Put the nails through the plates and into the holes with a tiny dab of glue on them, and spread a thin layer of glue under the ends of the cover. Flatten the cover down tight, wipe off the excess glue, put a weight on the harp and leave it alone till it sets.

If none of these ideas works, get another harp--but at least you tried. Again, if you got a big expensive chromatic it's probably worth a trip to a repair shop.

Another thing. Over a period of time the covers of harps that are soaked will get caved-in from being slapped out. A church key is good to open them up again with, but be sure that the point doesn't hit any reeds. Use one hand to hold down both ends of the harp cover while you pry in the middle of the harp with the other--if you're not cool, you can pry the whole cover off.

As far as any other suggestions for taking care of harps--I'd just say, don't drop them in the toilet, or let anyone with bubonic plague play them, or use them to load fists with or to carry pills in them.

Treat a harp right and it'll wear out anyhow... but you can make 'em last a little longer, with care.

Hammie Nixon, Sleepy John Estes and Yank Rachell (left to right). Nixon plays both harp and jug, and has recorded with Estes for over 30 years.

Photo by Raeburn Flerlage
Courtesy of Delmark Records

15

Amplified Harp

There are several ways to amplify harp--
both readymade and improvised. There are two
readymade "harmonica pick-ups"--consisting of a
holder with a built-in mike. The Kent model WC-17
sells for $12. It's a metal tube, with a lengthwise
slot cut into it, which the harp fits into--it's held by
two flanges at the edges of the slot. One end of the
tube has sound holes in it, in the other a crystal mike
with an external volume control knob is mounted.

The other model is Hohner HH9911, which
sells for $20. The mike is mounted in a molded
rubber piece, shaped like a triangle with the corners
rounded off some. The mike, again a crystal, is
mounted in the middle of this, and the harp is held
on by means of straps and a rubber band.

I don't like either one of these much for
blues, though they're probably good for other styles.
The Kent tube gives a nice tonal quality, but a good
deal is lost because it was designed for a bigger harp
than the small Marine Band (the bigger models #1816
and #365 fit well--so do 10-and 12-hole chromatics)--
and much of the sound escapes around the edges of
the larger slot. The mike is not the best and since
it's mounted on one end it tends to slightly over-
emphasize or distort the tones nearer to it. The
Hohner model with the mike in the middle tends to
over emphasize the middle range and drop off notes
on either end of the harp...and both are rather cum-
bersome, especially on gigs-unstrapping a harp can
get to be a drag when you're swinging.

Most harpmen prefer the "Chicago" method
of just cupping a PA mike in your hand along with the

James Cotton - Another Chicago harpman who has   Photo courtesy of M. Hohner
worked with Muddy Waters off and on for years.

harp. This way the harp is free to move in relation to the mike, so that the holes used are always near it to pick up correctly. Also some slight hand effects ("wah-wah's" etc.) are possible with a hand-held mike which are totally nonpossible with a harp strapped into a mike holder.

I've seen all kinds of mikes used. Some prefer using a contact mike and feeding it through a high power amp. Contacts run about $8--but they give a distorted tone. Most of the professional R&B harpmen use regular PA type mikes which range around $30 or so. The main thing to remember is that you get what you pay for. You'll be playing only about an inch or two from the mike, so you'll want one that doesn't "blast" easily, and you'll need durability. Crystal mikes are cheap, dynamics cost more, but they're worth it, since they're not sensitive to temperature extremes and take more banging around than the crystal mikes.

My own favorite is the Kent model DM-21, which sells for about $16. It's a dynamic mike, has a frequency range of 80-10,000 cycles (which is enough for most uses), it doesn't distort even at close range with full volume playing, and it's small and light (3 1/2" long) so that it's almost as if you were playing without a mike--it doesn't weigh you down. It comes with a 20-foot cord. And so far it's the most durable mike I've had yet.

Your best bet is to experiment around and find the model that you're most comfortable with, that you can afford, and that gives the sound you need. But remember that you're better off to buy one slightly expensive mike rather than three cheap ones.

As far as amplifiers go, I've seen everything from portable radios to huge hi-fi sets used. Most of the pro's use their own amps, for harp alone. If you plan to share an amp with anybody be sure that your channel has it's own tone and volume controls. If you can afford your own amp, try to get one with a "reverb" unit which gives distant, echolike effect, which works beautifully with the R&B sound. A "tremolo" effect is like vibration and not much use for bluesharp. Once again, buy what you need. If you'll be playing with a fully-amplified band you'll need a big amp with big speakers--they range from $150-$400 or more. On the other ear, if you'll only be playing with a single guitarist you can probably get by with a single channel amp without any special effects--these run from $30 on up. Best bet is for you to check out amps at a dealer--but insist on trying them with the mike you'll be using to see if it'll do what you want.

Once again, buy what you need--a six channel amp with oscillating speakers and neon lights is a little ridiculous and more than you'll need--but it's your bread baby, blow as thou pleaseth.

Kidney I (I don't dig appendixes at all)

Guitar/Harp Relationships

QUICK REFERENCE CHARTS

Like the title says, this section is mainly for reference--don't try to absorb it all at once. The only table you'll really need to know to begin with is the one for crossed harp in standard tuning--that's the one most frequently used.

STANDARD TUNING -- CONCERT PITCH

The E strings are tuned to E, and the others in the usual fashion--i.e. E-A-D-G-B-E.

FIRST OR STRAIGHT POSITION

Use a harp tuned in the same key that the guitar is playing.

SECOND or CROSSED POSITION

Use a harp tuned five steps (on the chromatic scale) above the key that the guitar is playing. Or, use a harp of the same tuning as the subdominant chord for the guitar key.

Guitar	Harp
E	A
A	D
G	C
D	G
C	F
F	B-flat
B	E

THIRD POSITION

(Use a harp tuned two steps below (on the chromatic scale) the key that the guitar is playing. In this position the key of F-natural isn't possible--however if the guitar is capoed one fret and F fingering patterns are used the actual pitch becomes F#--which is possible.)

Guitar	Harp
E	D
A	G
G	F
D	C
C	B-flat
B	A
____	____
F#	E

FOURTH POSITION

(Use a harp tuned four steps below (on the chromatic scale) the key that the guitar is playing in. In this position the keys of G, C and F-natural can't be accompanied unless a capo is placed on the first fret and the usual fingering patterns are used.)

Guitar	Harp
E	C
A	F
D	B-flat
B	G
____	____
G#	E
C#	A
F#	D

Lazy Lester - Louisiana bluesman who records solo and with Lightning Slim.   Photo courtesy of Chris Strachwitz

"LOW" AND OTHER TUNINGS

Some guitar players prefer to keep their strings tuned below concert pitch, so as to lessen the tension on the guitar neck and top, but as long as the same relative relationship is kept (that is, so that the intervals remain the same as in the concert tuning of E-A-D-G-B-E), low tunings can be accompanied with a harp.

Remember that the harp to be used is determined by the actual pitch of the chord--not by the fingering position. (In D tuning, for example, the strings have the same relative relationships, but one tone down (D-G-C-F-A-D)...the same intervals are kept but the whole setup is a tone lower. A guitar in D, when played with E fingering works--but an E chord has an actual pitch of D...and this is true of all other chord positions in this tuning; an A chord has an actual pitch of G, D becomes C and so on.) But no matter what tunings or fingering patterns are used, only one thing determines the harp to be used-- the <u>actual</u> <u>pitch</u> of the chord.

Here are the rules: FIRST POSITION--the harp is always the <u>same key</u> as the actual pitch of the chord.

SECOND POSITION--the harp is always tuned <u>five steps higher</u> on the chromatic scale than the actual pitch of the chord.

THIRD POSITION--the harp is always tuned <u>two steps lower</u> on the chromatic scale than the actual pitch of the chord.

FOURTH POSITION--the harp is always tuned <u>four steps lower</u> on the chromatic scale than the actual pitch of the chord.

Knowing this, once you know the actual pitch of a chord (find the note with a harp, guitar, whatever) it becomes simply a matter of counting to determine which harp to use to accompany in any position. And this works for any tuning in which the usual intervals such as E-A-D-G-B-E are kept.

However, putting all this counting into practice while you're trying to play is a drag--I find it's much easier to go by fingering patterns of the guitar man. So in the tables below, the keys listed under "guitar" are the fingering positions used--all the necessary adjustments have been made for you-- so all you have to know is which tuning is being used. Check the fingering position and the harp listed opposite it will be the correct one for the actual pitch of the chord.

"D" TUNING

(The guitar strings are tuned to the same intervals, but all one tone down from concert pitch. Notice that in both this and C tuning, the first position harp keys are the actual pitch of the guitar chords.)

FIRST POSITION

Guitar	Harp
E	D
A	G
D	C
G	F
B	A
C	B-flat
———	———
F#	E

SECOND or CROSSED POSITION

Guitar	Harp
E	G
A	C
D	F
G	B-flat
B	D
———	———
C#	E
F#	A

THIRD POSITION

Guitar	Harp
E	C
A	F
D	B-flat
B	G
———	———
G#	E
C#	A
F#	D

FOURTH POSITION

Guitar	Harp
E	B-flat
B	F
———	———
A#	E
D#	A
G#	D
C#	G
F#	C

SECOND or CROSSED POSITION

Guitar	Harp
E	F
A	B-flat
B	C
———	———
D#	E
G#	A
C#	D
F#	G

"C" TUNING

The same situation as D tuning, only all strings are tuned two full tones (four half-steps) below concert pitch. In this tuning the actual pitch of any chord is four steps below the fingering position used. Remember, though, this has been compensated for--the harp listed is the correct one for the fingering position listed under the guitar heading. This tuning is most often used by 12-string guitarists who don't like the gnashing, tearing sound of a guitar splintering into sharded shreds. Note that in this tuning a capo is often necessary.

THIRD POSITION

Guitar	Harp
E	B-flat
B	F
———	———
A#	E
D#	A
G#	D
C#	G
F#	C

FIRST POSITION

Guitar	Harp
E	C
A	F
D	B-flat
B	G
———	———
G#	E
C#	A
F#	D

FOURTH POSITION

(Capo on first fret necessary for all keys.)

Guitar	Harp
E#	A
A#	D
D#	G
G#	C
C#	F
F#	B-flat
B#	E

MINOR TUNINGS

Rots-A-Ruck. You oughta know better than to play blues in minor keys anyway.

OPEN TUNINGS

An open tuning is one where the guitar is tuned to a chord--if you strum it you get a chord without fretting any strings. The most common open tunings in blues are E and A...however, most guitar players, rather than tighten the strings up to an E or A chord, usually drop the other strings down--which gives a relative E or A chord (it has the same intervals) even though the actual pitch usually is D and G, respectively.

Once you know the actual pitch all you have to do is go back to the charts for standard tuning. For example, an open E relative chord, with an actual pitch of D is the same as a guitar played in D--so you'd accompany in second position with a G harp.

Any other open tunings (as long as they're major chords and not something like a C# diminished to the 9th power) work the same way. Just find the actual pitch, then treat them like usual keys in standard tuning.

HARP POSITIONS--BASIC PATTERNS

These are repeated for quick reference. An arrow pointing down means draw, an arrow pointing up means blow--and the number is the hole used.

FIRST POSITION

tonic	subdominant	dominant
4 ↑	5 ↓	3 ↑

SECOND (CROSSED) POSITION

tonic	subdominant	dominant
2 ↓	4 ↑	4 ↓

THIRD POSITION

tonic	subdominant	dominant
4 ↓	3 ↑	6 ↓

FOURTH POSITION

tonic	subdominant	dominant
2 ↑	6 ↓	3 ↓

SHARPS AND FLATS IN HARPS

A harp tuned in the key in the left hand column will have certain built in sharps and/or flats...this table shows which. Handy to use if you ever need a C# note.

KEY	SHARPS OR FLATS
E	C# D# F# G#
A	C# F# G#
D	C# F#
G	F#
C	none
F	B flat
B flat	B flat, E flat

Detroit bluesman, Isiah "Doctor" Ross makes up-to-the-minute blues with harmonica and electric guitar. Born in the south, he now lives in Flint, Mich., and appears in clubs in the Detroit area.   Photo courtesy of M. Hohner

Kidney II

A list of books related to blues follows. Each has some good things in it, and as a sum will help you get a better understanding of the overall blues scene.

THE MEANING OF THE BLUES by Paul Oliver Collier Books, AS 497V. Paper, $.95. To date, This is the most complete and accurate book about the blues. It focuses on the meanings and backgrounds of the blues, rather than on individual singers. Some may find the sociological going a little heavy, but it's well worth wading through. Many blues verses are used as illustrations, and a discography is given.

THE STORY OF JAZZ, by Marshall Stearns. Mentor Books, MD 240. Paper, $.50. Though mostly devoted to jazz, this book covers in depth the backgrounds common to both blues and jazz, and has a good deal of technical and historical musical data worth knowing. An extensive bibliography is included.

THE COUNTRY BLUES, by Sam Charters. Rhinehart & Co. Hardcover, $4.95. By now much of this book is largely outdated: much of the information and many of the speculations have been proved incorrect, and many singers presumed dead have since been rediscovered. Nonetheless, this is the book that helped pave the way for many of the rediscoveries, and is still worth reading. It's a surface survey of the blues, concerned with individual bluesmen, with chapters devoted to Blind Willie Johnson, Big Bill, Muddy Waters, Lightnin' Hopkins, etc. It also covers the development of the commercial blues scene.

THE POETRY OF THE BLUES, by Sam Charters. Oak Publications. Paper, $1.95. This book focuses on the blues as academic literature, and is of more interest to students than to fans. But it does have some nice photographs of older bluesmen such as J.D. Short and Pink Anderson.

BEEN HERE AND GONE, by Frederick Ramsey Jr. Rutgers University Press. Hardcover, $5.00. This is largely a photographic essay of the Negro south and the land of the blues. The text is sometimes awkward, but the many excellent pictures are worth more than several thousand words (To coin a phrase). This book is almost a poem in pictures and beautifully illustrates the places that gave birth to the blues, and the almost anonymous people who gave them life.

BIG BILL BLUES, by Yannick Bruynoghe. Oak Publications. Paper, $2.95. This is Big Bill Broonzy's autobiography, and contains several of his songs as well as a lot of stories about himself and his blues singing friends--which are interesting, if not always true.

THE LEADBELLY SONGBOOK. Oak Publications, paper $1.95. The story of Leadbelly with much of his music (as written for him by the Lomaxes).

There are many books about folk music in general which have references to blues in them. You should be able to hunt them down without trouble at your library. However, a definitive book about the blues has yet to be written....

Kidney III

The LP's listed below all have harp on them, and all should be easily available. The order is roughly chronological. Where an artist has many LP's on the market, only my favorites are listed.

REALLY! THE COUNTRY BLUES. Origin Jazz Library, OJL-2. (39 Remsen St. (1E) Brooklyn Heights 1, N.Y.)
Contains one cut (TOUCH ME LIGHT MAMA) by George "Bullet" Williams worth the price of the whole LP.

THE GREAT JUG BANDS. Origin Jazz Library, OJL-4. Ten of the fifteen cuts have harp on them by people like Noah Lewis, Will Shade, Jaybird Coleman and others. This is a fine sampling of jug-band styled harp.

SLEEPY JOHN ESTES, 1929-40. RBF 8.
Four of the twelve cuts have the harp of Hammie Nixon with John. More recent work of both can be found on various Delmark LP's (Delmark Records, 7 West Grand, Chicago 10, Ill.).

LEADBELLY MEMORIAL, VOL. I. Stinson, SLP 17.
Five of the twelve cuts have Sonny Terry at his best.

LEADBELLY SINGS FOLK SONGS. Folkways, FA 2488. Three cuts with Sonny Terry--and a groovy OUTSKIRTS OF TOWN.

CHAIN GANG BLUES, VOL. I & II. Stinson, SLPX 7. Sonny Terry with Woody Guthrie and Alec Stewart. Contains a great version of LOST JOHN.

HARMONICA & VOCAL SOLOS. Folkways, FP 35.
A 10" LP with some fine solo work by Sonny Terry.

POSSUM UP A SIMMON TREE. Folk-Lyric, FL 107.
Snooks Eaglin's vocal and guitar backed by the folk country harp of Percy Randolph on six of the fifteen cuts.

J.D. SHORT & SON HOUSE. Folkways, FA 2467.
Short has one side of this LP to himself, playing both harp and guitar.

STAVIN CHAIN BLUES. Delmark 609. J.D. Short's mournful harp with his own vocals and accompanying guitar vocal work by Big Joe Williams.

JESSE FULLER. Good Time Jazz 12031. The one-man band-with harp and kazoo.

SONNY BOY WILLIAMSON (I) Blues Classics, 3 (Box 5073 Berkeley 5, Calif.). The backing ranges from guitars to a full band. The beginnings of R&B.

SONNY BOY WILLIAMSON (Rice Miller) Blues Classics 9. 16 cuts featuring the harp and vocals of the "original" Sonny Boy at the peak of his form with full driving energy. MIGHTY LONG TIME is worth the price of the whole LP....beg borrow or steal, but GET THIS SIDE!
(Although the title listed may not be used, you can order by number--release date is set for fall, 1965.)

DOWN AND OUT BLUES. Checker, LP 1437.
Sonny Boy Williamson II with a sampling of R&B from the mid-fifties.

THE BLUES ROLL ON. Atlantic 1352. Four cuts by Forest City Joe (who patterned himself after the Sonny Boy I) and two by a harpman called Boy Blue. Both with country R&B backing.

THE BEST OF LITTLE WALTER. Chess 1428.
Twelve cuts--four of them instrumental. A good sampling of Chicago R&B. Walter also accompanies Muddy Waters on THE BEST OF MUDDY WATERS Chess LP 1427 on several cuts.

ROOSTER BLUES. Excello 80000.
The harp of Lazy Lester with vocals by Lightning Slim. R&B gone back to Louisiana.

HOWLING WOLF: MOANING IN THE MOONLIGHT. Chess 1434.
Wolf plays funky harp with down-home backing on all twelve cuts.

JIMMY REED: THE LEGEND AND THE MAN. Vee-Jay 8501.
Twelve cuts, eleven with the "high head harp" by the master of lazy Chicago blues.

This list is by no means complete, but it covers a pretty thorough span of styles and time. Dig all of them and you'll have heard a lot of the best.

In Back

A few last thoughts.

For too long now there have been all kinds of arguments as to whether or not a man who didn't grow up with the blues has a right to try to play them.

I think that's about as stupid as saying that an American shouldn't learn how to speak French, or that only Italians should sing opera. Once a language is made, anybody who can speak it right has the right to use it--especially the language of music. There shouldn't be any bars or walls on any sides. Music is like the air--it should belong to everybody. There's only one thing--if you didn't grow up with the blues, remember that you're speaking somewhat of a foreign language, and there's no sense in trying to con anybody into thinking you're a native. Just be you, speaking well in a language you dig.

You can add to the language, turn your own phrases, maybe make some of your own forms--just remember that you're adding onto a foundation that has already been laid, and if you want your additions to fit in, they should be in the same form. Putting a steeple on a ranch-style rambler would be a wig, true, but it wouldn't be a rambler house anymore, and you wouldn't fool anybody by saying it still is.

One last thing. In December, 1963, Time magazine did a piece on the Kweskin Jug Band, interviewing some of the members, including the harpman, Mel Lyman. But he was (of course) quoted wrong. What he actually said was "When I play, I am a mouthharp...people who play the harmonica are hung up."

And that's just about where it's at.

But you won't learn how to get your head to that place from any book--except the book of your own life.

And the time to start writing it is now.

Go thou and blow now.

Mpls...May, 1965

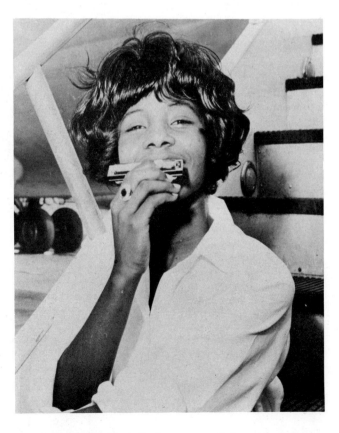

Millie Small - She doesn't actually play blues harp, but it's a groovy picture.

Photo courtesy of M. Hohner

And now, for all these imaginative, groovy blowers who are looking for a way to be the life of the party, we pass along some tips taken from an old-time harmonica instruction method.

HOW TO SECURE A BEAUTIFUL TONE

Study the illustration to the left carefully. Place a glass tumbler over the right end of the Harmonica and against the cheek. By moving the glass in a very slow shaking movement the tone is enhanced to a great degree.

HOW TO PLAY TWO HARMONICAS AT ONE TIME

AN AMUSING NOVELTY EFFECT!

Play Harmonica Through a Hose

FIRST:

Use two single reed Harmonicas in the same key. Hold one Harmonica in each hand, so that the high notes are toward the palms of your hands. Place the instrument in your left hand to your lips so that part of the Harmonica protrudes from your mouth. See illustration. Play gently for several seconds.

Position of Harmonica When Placing in Mouth

SECOND:

Then very quickly remove from your mouth the instrument in your left hand, and at the same instant slip into position the Harmonica which you are holding in your right hand. Try not to interrupt what you are playing.

Alternate the two instruments as frequently as you wish but keep correct time.

Use any single reed Harmonica.

Procure four feet of rubber tubing one-half inch in diameter.

Place one end of the tube in your mouth between your teeth. Bring the other end over your left shoulder, around behind your neck and down over your right shoulder. Grasp this end firmly between the thumb and forefinger of your right hand.

Lay the Harmonica flat on the palm of your left hand, placing the instrument so that the low notes are toward your wrist.

Now place the end of the tube, which you are holding between the thumb and forefinger of your right hand, directly over any hole of the Harmonica that you wish to play. After you can blow or draw one hole clearly, move the end of the tube gently up and down the Harmonica, playing other notes in the same way. Lastly, try playing some tune

HOW TO PLAY UP AND DOWN

Use any Harmonica.

Place the instrument close to your lips, but in an upright position. The bass notes are downward, the higher notes upward.

Blow and draw gently, until by moving the Harmonica up and down you can play all the notes clearly. Then play a melody.

Remember — you must keep the Harmonica tightly pressed against your lips.

HOW TO PLAY WHILE DANCING

With adhesive and some ordinary elastic, make a Harmonica holder which will slip over your head and hold your instrument fairly well in place.

With this device, two people can execute any kind of partner dance, folk dance, reel or jig, playing their own accompaniment as they do so.

The use of castanets adds greatly to a dance performed by a Harmonica player.

ANOTHER NOVELTY EFFECT

Use any single reed Harmonica.

Practice holding the Harmonica in your mouth for short intervals without the aid of your hands.

Next try arm movements, sideward, upward and forward while playing, bringing the hands back to the Harmonica in rhythm.

Next practice bending the trunk forward, holding the Harmonica in your mouth without the aid of your hands, and playing as you bend.

By combining marching, marking time, free exercises of arms and legs, trunk bending, etc., with Harmonica playing, a very interesting effect can be produced.

HOW TO PLAY HARMONICA THROUGH YOUR EAR

"Palm "Little Lady" Harmonica in Left Hand

Use a "Little Lady" Harmonica and also a larger instrument. Conceal the tiny Harmonica in the palm of your left hand.

Then casually pass your hand over your mouth, placing the little instrument well inside your mouth.

SLIP SMALL HARMONICA INTO MOUTH

Next take the large Harmonica in your right hand and place it across your right ear.

Before executing the actual trick, you should breathe very hard several times to make it appear extremely difficult to force your breath out through your ear.

When the audience is sufficiently impressed, play something on the tiny Harmonica concealed in your mouth.

It sometimes helps to introduce this trick with a scientific explanation of the air passages between the nose and ear.

HOW TO PLAY HARMONICA UNDER A GLASS

Use any Harmonica, although a 34-B is best.

Procure an ordinary drinking glass.

Place the harmonica well inside your mouth, your tongue against the lower or bass notes, and allow the upper half of the instrument to protrude from your mouth.

Then take the glass and invert it over the Harmonica between your nose and chin, balancing it by tilting your head well back.

By moving your tongue up and down over the bass notes, while inhaling and exhaling or blowing and drawing, the desired effect will be produced. Play "Home, Sweet Home" for this trick.

Index